THE SECRET PLOT TO
KILL HITLER

Hitler showing Mussolini the damage caused by Stauffenberg's bomb.

◀IVIRTUAL HISTORY▶▶

The Secret Plot to Kill

HITLER

DUNJA NOACK

This edition published under license from Discovery Communications, Inc. in 2005 by Cerberus Publishing ltd.

Cerberus Publishing Limited
22A Osprey Court
Hawkfield Business Park
Bristol BS14 0BB
UK
Tel: +44 (0) 1275 54 54 70
Fax: +44 (0) 1275 54 54 72
e-mail:cerberusbooks@aol.com
www.cerberus-publishing.com

British Library Cataloguing in Publication Data.
A catalogue record for this book is available from the British Library.

ISBN 1 84145 016 2

PRINTED AND BOUND IN THE UNITED STATES OF AMERICA.

Contents

		Page
Acknowledgments		*vii*
Introduction		*ix*
CHAPTER ONE	The Good German	1
CHAPTER TWO	Weapons of Mass Destruction	17
CHAPTER THREE	The Supreme War Lord	33
CHAPTER FOUR	Inside the Wolf's Lair	47
CHAPTER FIVE	The Dying President	59
CHAPTER SIX	Arming the Bomb	73
CHAPTER SEVEN	A Bomb Explodes	87
CHAPTER EIGHT	Don't Tell Dr Bruenn	101
CHAPTER NINE	Providence	121
CHAPTER TEN	Your Enemy's Enemy	137
CHAPTER ELEVEN	To Win the War	153
CHAPTER TWELVE	Long Live Sacred Germany	167
Appendix	The Making of Virtual History	183
Bibliography		189

To my exceptionally patient
and loving husband

Acknowledgments

I AM grateful to so many people for their support, friendship, knowledge and professionalism in making this project possible, both the book and the film with which it is associated.

At Discovery it could not have happened without the faith, persistence and undying support of David Abraham, who went through all the deep valleys with us, and helped us reach the final summit. At Tiger Aspect Productions our indomitable Line Producer Sarah Sapper, kept us on the straight and narrow – while administering chocolate cookies and a bright smile. My gratitude also goes to David McNab for giving invaluable advice.

The film would not have been possible without the four men who volunteered to embark on a new way of bringing history to life: Clive Brooks (Hitler), Gerry George (Churchill), Dickie Richards (FDR), and Vic Chester (Stalin).

The production team behind virtual history was truly exceptional: Charlotte Malik, who designed our beautiful sets; Joe Taylor, our DoP who gave the film the authentic home movie look; Joe Hobbs, who made everyone of our cast look like a true 1940s person; and Chrissie Webster, our make-up designer, who made our actors look like their historic counterparts; our film researcher Aileen McAllister, who found the most astonishing archive; and Jim Meacock for composing an outstanding score. We went through three editors: our thanks go to David Fairhead, Dan Glendenning, and Peter Cartwright. And then there were two wonderful people without whom we would have been lost, because they looked after all our production and research needs: Elaine Foster and Kasie Moore. And a final thanks to Brendan Kilcawley for putting up with this erratic German producer.

At The Moving Picture Company Jim Radford not only accepted the challenge of 'rebuilding Hitler' but persisted with it … thanks to Oliver Money – who not only managed the VFX team excellently but had patience with the client.

My thanks go to Antony Buonomo and Piers Wallace at Vertigo

– who created our 2D stills and graphic designs, and brought Stauffenberg back to life, for the film and the book.

An enormous thanks to Sara Hill, Todd Dalton, Blair Wallace and Phil Reed at Arena/P3, who not only made the film look slick, beautifully coloured, and sounding like a million dollars, but also sacrificed many weekends and evenings to bring it together.

Finally, my thanks go to my agent Sandy Holton at Curtis Brown for supporting this first time author, Colin West at Cerberus for believing in this book, Melisa Bunce at Discovery for bringing the deal together, and Le Saint Geran on Mauritius for endless inspiration.

Introduction

TWO years ago, the development research started for our documentary film project 'virtual history' for Discovery Channel. We wanted to recreate one day in the Second World War that had significance for all four war leaders. Days were spent reading at Colindale Newspaper Library in London, when I came across the following headlines:

England hit by Heaviest Robot Attack
Fuehrer burned, bruised by Bomb Blast
Roosevelt Nominated for a Record 4th Term
Russians drive into the Heart of Poland

These were the main headlines of one day. It was the 20th July 1944. The headlines are from the New York Times. History writes the best scripts, and this day had it all:

A powerful bomb rips through Adolf Hitler's East Prussian Headquarters during a briefing which he attends with his senior advisors. Miraculously, the bomb planted by a German Colonel fails to kill Hitler. The bomb is part of a wider conspiracy of the German army to overthrow the Nazi Régime from within. At the end of this day, the conspirators learn the bitter lesson, that neither the American President nor the British Prime Minister are keen for Hitler to die now, or to support the army rebellion.

This day does not only have a major bomb plot, it also features the story of President Franklin D Roosevelt, who on this day, frail and terminally ill, comes close to death himself, and collapses on the floor only hours before being nominated for a record 4th term.

London experiences the heaviest night of V1 bombardment and a beleaguered Winston Churchill considers dropping poison gas on German civilians in retaliation. Clearly, he has reached a level of desperation which his close advisors fear colours his judgement.

On this same day, in his dacha near Moscow, the Soviet Premier and supreme warlord Josef Stalin instructs his troops to install a puppet regime in liberated Poland. Poland will be the cornerstone of his emerging Soviet Empire.

Together with Discovery Channel we decided that our film 'virtual history' would recreate the historic drama of this day. The idea was to take the dramatic concept of the popular television drama series '24', which we would adapt to a real day in history. Our film was going to recreate the 24 hours and recreate the minutiae of this one day. The aim was to use the immediacy the drama series has, but translate it to history television.

To further enhance the feeling of watching 'history as it happens', we decided to use computer graphics to wrap computer animated faces of the four war leaders around the modern-day actors who were re-enacting the day in dramatic reconstructions. Jim Radford of The Moving Picture Company explains in 'Making of Virtual History' chapter how we achieved this technically. To create 'virtual history' we filmed all our dramatic reconstructions in the style of 1940s amateur home movie footage, which was film effected in post-production in such a way that this new 'virtual history archive' now blends in seamlessly in with the real historic archive.

This book follows the same principles as the film. It tells the twenty-four hours of this day following the simultaneous story-lines as they unfold. It tries to give a glimpse into the very personal routines of the four war leaders and their leadership-style: Churchill conducting the war from his bed; Hitler receiving his daily drug injections; Stalin cavorting with his housekeeper Valetchka, and Roosevelt renewing his love affair with Lucy Mercer Rutherford. This might serve as a timely look at past leaders in order to compare them with the war-time leaders of our time.

I hope that the reader will feel the same sensation I felt reading the headlines on that day in Colindale, a sense of immediacy. Often when we look at history, we do this with the hindsight of knowing how it all ended. But on the 20th July 1944, nobody knew for sure how it all would end. This book is a snapshot, not a comprehensive history of the Second World War, – hopefully an insightful and thought-provoking snapshot.

London, December 2004.

CHAPTER ONE

0700 Hours – Berlin

The Good German

The point is no longer to tell Hitler the truth but to get rid of him.

Stauffenberg, 1943

IT is 0700hours on Thursday, the 20th July, 1944. Rangsdorf Military airfield – south-east of the German capital Berlin. After a long night of air raids and Allied bombings, the beginning of another bright summer day. The summer of 1944 is particularly hot and beautiful. In the sixth year of the war, Berliners – famous for their sharp-witted humour – coined a new joke commenting on the good summer of this now sixth year of the war: 'Enjoy the war – peace will be horrible.'

On this bright morning, two men are setting off in a Heinkel He 111 plane which will take them from Berlin to Adolf Hitler's secret Field Head Quarters near the Eastern Front, the so-called Wolf's Lair, hidden deep in the East Prussian forest. Colonel Count von Stauffenberg is with his adjutant Lieutenant Werner von Haeften. Stauffenberg has recently been promoted to Chief of Staff to the Commander of the German Reserve Army, General Friedrich Fromm. Today he has been summoned by Hitler to report to him personally on a timetable for raising fresh troops to fight the massive onslaught by the Red Army in the East. In his briefcase, Stauffenberg carries a thick report on reserve troops – and four pounds of explosives. Today, Stauffenberg plans to assassinate Adolf Hitler.

It has been six weeks since the Western Allies have landed on the shores of Normandy. Hitler famously rejoiced at the prospect of being able to fight his 'enemies' now on continental Europe, his 'home turf'. But while Hitler welcomed the invasion, Germany's generals and officers despaired. Convinced that all is lost Field Marshal Erwin Rommel – Nazi Germany's most admired military leader and until then utterly loyal to the Führer – twice begged

Von Stauffenberg and von Haeften flying from Berlin to the Wolf's Lair. (Reconstruction)

Hitler in June 1944 to draw the proper conclusions from the Normandy landings and end the war immediately.

Rommel is not alone. Many German Generals are painfully aware of the fact that their forces are now stretched to the absolute limit. They are trying to fight off a materially far superior enemy in the West – one million men, 170,000 vehicles and over 500,000 tons of material have been shipped across the Channel – while at the same time desperately withstanding the Soviet Union's own Blitzkrieg. To coincide with the D-Day landings, Stalin unleashed 'Operation Bagration' on 23 June, 1944. Two and a half million Soviet soldiers are driving the German army out of Nazi-occupied White Russia and are advancing at lightning speed. The skill and speed of the offensive proves that the Red Army is now tactically and operationally superior to the German Wehrmacht. Hitler has yet to fight a war under pressure and his desperate lack of imagination is reflected in the feeble tactical advice he gives to his troops: 'fight to the last'.

It doesn't help the Wehrmacht that the Allied troops are also advancing from the South through Italy. The classic pincer movement serves to put further pressure on the manpower and resources of the German army in July 1944. To many of them it is clear that Germany is losing the war, but Hitler refuses to accept it.

Defying his oath of allegiance, Colonel Claus von Stauffenberg is about to commit the ultimate act of betrayal. But what kind of soldier would kill his supreme commander in times of war?

Claus was born into a baronial family of Swabian aristocrats in Southern Germany. His father was Lord Chamberlain to the King of Württemberg. On 15th November, 1907, his mother in her eighth month of pregnancy gave birth to a pair of boy twins, Konrad and Claus. Konrad died a day after the birth. When Claus was old enough to be told about his lost twin, he lamented his loss. For a time he often brought his mother flowers for his twin brother's grave.[1]

Of staunch Catholic background, Claus and his two elder brothers enjoyed a traditional aristocratic childhood in Imperial Germany, spent between holidays in the Alps, teas with the Royal Family, and a busy salon run by their mother.[2] All was well until 31 July, 1914. Men and boys from the Stauffenberg village had to

Field Marshal
Erwin Rommel

[2] P Hoffmann, op. cit., p.7.
[1] Peter Hoffmann, *Stauffenberg*, 2003, p.2.

return home from their summer holidays. Claus' mother, the children, their Irish governess Miss Barry and the servants returned to their official residence in Stuttgart. The First World War had begun.

Count Alfred von Stauffenberg with his sons Berthold, Claus and, seated, Alex.

Field hospitals were set up, air raid alerts sounded, wounded soldiers were walking the streets amidst great general public interest; announcements of victories were made. Miss Barry, who only spoke English, could no longer go out with the children. As enemy alien, she had to report twice daily to the police. Countess von Stauffenberg was dismayed about the war. But her sons reacted quite differently to the war. They were seized by the general enthusiasm, and Claus – now almost seven years old – prayed every evening that the soldiers would come home again, all the wounded be healed, and every fallen soldier would go to heaven.[3]

But most soldiers would not return home, and when Germany requested an armistice on October 3rd, 1918, Claus was in tears and said 'my Germany cannot perish; if she goes down now, she will rise again strong and great, after all there is still a God.' Amidst the revolutionary movements in Stuttgart, the King of Württemberg abdicated and November 15th, 1918 became the saddest birthday in young Claus' life. For the Stauffenberg family a tradition going back many generations came to an end. For centuries they had served reigning monarchs as noble vassals and had themselves lorded over farmers and servants. Now it was the people who ruled. The thought of being the servants of the people was a strange one to them.[4]

The trauma of the lost war and the loss of a system of values bore heavy on the Stauffenberg boys. Claus grew up in a Germany dominated by economic hardship, inflation, and political turmoil. More than anything the 'shame of the Treaty of Versailles' incensed the young generation. Claus and his elder brothers joined the Catholic mysticism and romantic circle around the German poet Stefan George. Within this circle, Claus often spoke of the 'painful birth of a new Germany, of national duty and service'.[5]

Stefan George with Berthold and Claus von Stauffenberg.

Claus dreamed from a very early age about becoming a soldier. On April 1st, 1926, he joined the No.17 Cavalry Regiment in Bamberg and attended the Infantry School in Dresden. His

[3] P Hoffmann, op. cit., p.7.
[4] P Hoffmann, op. cit., p.14.
[5] P Hoffmann, op. cit., p.45.

*Count Claus von
Stauffenberg as a young
cavalry officer.*

slightly untidy dress and bearing, and his irresistible laughter, mislead some people about his uncompromising allegiance to everything that he regarded as fundamental: Germany, truthfulness, and a romantic notion of leadership. Stauffenberg wanted to be a 'Good German' and to him that meant total loyalty to Germany. In his free time, he began to learn Russian. In the evenings he played the cello, and read widely from the *Odyssey*, in Greek, to military books on annihilation strategies.[6] All through his military training he excelled. In the examination for an officer's commission, Stauffenberg was placed first on the list of officer cadets, and returned home as second lieutenant.[7]

But by the early 1930s, Stauffenberg's beloved Germany was yet at another crossroads. Political parties were fractioned into

[6] P Hoffmann, op. cit., p.49.
[7] P Hoffmann, op. cit., p. 51

splinter-groups and the Weimar Republic was at the brink of disintegrating, when former Field-Marshal von Hindenburg was elected as President of the Republic. In this position he was the key to nominating the Chancellor of the Republic. And, under pressure, he appointed Adolf Hitler as Chancellor on January 30th 1933, as leader of a coalition government. To many Germans this was just another coalition doomed to fail. But some saw in Hitler the long-hoped-for National Resurgence, while many others feared he was going to plunge Germany into the abyss.

As a soldier, Claus could not vote in the 1933 elections. But he often expressed his support for Hitler during social gatherings.

Stauffenberg with two of his children.

Fellow officers described him as nationalist and politically right-wing – like all officers. Claus was enthusiastic about Hitler's 'national' movement. He supported re-armament, expansion of the Army, acquisition of heavy weapons – all forbidden under the terms of the Treaty of Versailles. He also supported Hitler's goal of unifying all national Germans within the borders of the Reich. A relative of his wife Nina recalls the family's surprise at Claus' later involvement in the assassination attempt of 20th July, 1944 – many thought of Claus as the only real National Socialist in the family.[8]

In 1933 – Hitler seemed to embody all the romantic ideals the 26-year old Stauffenberg had discussed with his poet tutor Stefan George, when the group of young men longed for moral renewal and national leadership.

Hitler for his part actively courted the officers of the German army. Only three days after his appointment as Chancellor on 3rd February, 1933, he made his way to the German Army Headquarters in the Bendlerstrasse in Berlin. The military commanders were reputed to be remote, secretive and arrogant, and Hitler went to the meeting with some trepidation, because he knew the army played a key role in his aims of seizing control of Germany and for his long-range plans of territorial expansion.[9] Hitler knew that the younger officers – like Stauffenberg – sympathized with him, but that senior officers took quite a different view. Hitler was persuasive and the top army officers succumbed to the prospects of increased rearmament and status, and adopted the Nazi insignia as the official symbol of the armed forces. Furthermore, under the statute of the emergency legislation which Hitler forced through in 1933, all officers and enlisted men were ordered to swear an oath of allegiance to their new supreme commander, the Führer Adolf Hitler. The wording of the oath violated the German constitution by requiring soldiers to swear unconditional obedience to Hitler personally. It was a fateful step, undermining the army's traditional role of political impartiality.[10]

Hitler wasted no time to ready Germany for war and on 1st September 1939 – Nazi Germany attacked Poland. In the afternoon, Stauffenberg's division was ordered to cross the border. Only three days later he witnessed as one of his officers had two Polish women shot out of hand without any investigation, on suspicion of having given signals to Polish artillery batteries. Stauffenberg, who had been on friendly terms with the officer, did not rest until he had been court-martialed and demoted.

[8] Interview P Hoffmann with M Lerchenfeld, 18 May 1989, P Hoffmann, op. cit., p. 69
[9] Joachim Fest, *Plotting Hitler's Death*, 1996, p.36.
[10] J Fest, op. cit., p.45 - 55.

*A formal portrait of
Count Claus von
Stauffenberg*

But the aggressive expansion continues and on 31st May, 1940, Stauffenberg, a rising star in the German Army was awarded the Iron Cross First Class for his tactical skills and bravery, and after his triumphs in the French campaign, he was transfered into the heart of the German war-machine, the General Staff.

Hitler's orders for the mass murder of Polish intellectuals, Jews, the mentally ill, and later of the political commissars of the Red Army were fairly well known at the highest level of the Army High Command. There is however no indication that Stauffenberg learned of the systematic mass killings before the spring of 1942, it is clear that during the first months of the Russian campaign, his attention was however drawn to the crimes committed by the SS and special police units behind the front lines.[11]

[11] He requested an officer to look into the matter and report to him any facts of SS atrocities. See P Hoffmann, op. cit., p. 112.

Summer 1941 – and Nazi Germany invades Soviet-occupied Poland. For many officers – the turning point in their attitude to Hitler and his military strategy. Even though Soviet Russia was the 'natural ideological enemy' of Nazi-Germany, many conservative officers agreed that to attack the Soviet Union was a strategic folly.

In April 1942 Stauffenberg expressed in private his outrage at the brutal treatment of the civilian population in the German-occupied Soviet Union, the mass murder 'of racially inferior' persons, especially the Jews, and the mass starvation and murder of Soviet prisoners-of-war in German custody. In May 1942, Stauffenberg received eye-witness reports of mass executions of Jews in the Ukraine. Upon hearing this report Stauffenberg said that Hitler must be removed. He believed, it was the senior commanders duty to put this into effect and overthrow the 'foolish and criminal' Führer.[12]

To the soldier in Stauffenberg – Hitler's campaign in the East showed that 'the supreme commander' did not possess the strategic leadership any longer that he expected of him. But what

Carl Goerdeler (left) and General Ludwig Beck

[12] P Hoffmann, op. cit., p.151

bore most heavily on the conscience of this morally upright man was the barbarity with which the war against Soviet Russia was fought. Furthermore, Stauffenberg, the officer, observed with despair how the denigrated ways of the SS were seeping into the mindset of his ordinary soldiers. Not only did Hitler endanger the material future of Stauffenberg's 'holy Germany' by embarking on dangerous military adventures, but Hilter's evil also started to erode the greater moral values of what to Stauffenberg was 'holy Germany'.

By spring 1943, the 'Good German' Claus von Stauffenberg will come to the notice of the men of the military resistance against Hitler.[13]

The German resistance against Hitler within Nazi Germany never existed in the sense of a unified group or movement sharing a common set of ideals. It was a cacophony of voices, from Catholic opponents to Hitler, to trade unionists, socialists and conservatives. Numerous groups existed, acting separately and often holding juxtaposed views.

But resistance there was. And of all the various resistance groups, three Conservative groups came to prominence, because they at least attempted to join forces and formulate a strategy to overthrow Hitler. They became a genuine threat to the Nazi régime: Firstly, there was the Conservative opposition around Carl Goerdeler – a former mayor of Leipzig, and General Ludwig Beck, who had resigned as army chief of staff after Hitler invaded Czechoslovakia in 1938. Then there was the so-called Kreisau Circle, named after the country estate of its leader Count Helmuth von Moltke – descendant of Field Marshal Moltke, who had led the German army to victory over France in 1870. The Kreisau Circle opposed the Nazi régime because of their firmly held Christian beliefs. And finally, there were the régime's opponents within the German military itself.

All three groups agreed that it was their duty to save as much of the 'substance' of Germany as possible from the political and moral corruption of the Nazis. They all agreed that it would be impossible to stage a people's uprising against the Nazi régime. Hitler enjoyed continued popularity among the masses – that is until the war against the Soviet Union started in 1941. And most of the army chiefs felt a sense of loyalty toward Hitler as their commander in chief. There was also a very real and existential fear of the awesome consequences of discovery of any complicity in a plot to remove the head of state. The terror machine of the Gestapo and the SS was by now working well.

[13] P Hoffmann, op. cit.. p. 187

The only viable option for the opposition was to use the position the conspirators had over the might of the German army and stage an armed military coup against the Nazi régime, and against their superior officers.

Lieutenant Werner von Haeften (left) and Count Helmuth von Moltke

Crucial to the success of such a coup however would be whether the Allies were willing to negotiate a peace with the renegade German generals after a successful coup. Since the summer of 1941 various attempts were made to get in touch through informal back channels in Sweden and Switzerland – to test the waters primarily with the Western Allies, Britain und the USA.[14]

But the replies coming back to the German conspirators were little encouraging. Churchill instructed 'perfect silence' to these German feelers. The British were concerned that entering into negotiations with Germans, even anti-Nazi Germans, would jeopardize their Alliance with the Soviet Union. This attitude was strengthened with the Casablanca declaration in January 1943, when Roosevelt and Churchill vowed that the Allies would 'continue the war relentlessly' until they achieved 'unconditional

[14] Allen Welsh Dulles, *Germany's Underground*, 1947/2000, p. 125 details all the German feelers sent out to the US and British governments.

surrender'. The cold-shoulder approach to the resistance was thus given the seal of official strategy by both governments.[15]

Casablanca was a serious blow to the renegade German generals. The policy of unconditional surrender led many to feel that to oppose Hitler would be to betray their own country, and only very few were prepared to go that far, especially in wartime.

The turning-point however was to be the surrender of the 6th Army under Field Marshal Paulus in Stalingrad in January 1943. The senseless slaughter of fellow soldiers because their supreme commander – Hitler – had issued the order to fight to the last man, incensed the military opposition, who now felt there was no more time to lose.

In the following weeks and months the anti-Hitler conspiracy among the military, feverishly sought to try to assassinate Hitler. Two assassination attempts in March 1943 failed. On 12th March, 1943 a bomb was smuggled on the Führer's plane, disguised as a Cognac bottle. But the low temperatures during the flight meant that the crude acid fuse mechanism of the bomb did not react. Hitler remained unharmed. On 21st March, 1943, Hitler was scheduled to inspect captured Soviet tanks – Count von Gersdorff was to blow himself up when Hitler was near him. But Hitler decided to cut the inspection short and survived yet another attempt.

Equally if not more important was, however, the question 'what do to once Hitler had been killed'. The military opposition had failed so far in coming up with a succinct plan. Conspirator Colonel General Friedrich Olbricht, former Chief of Staff to the Reserve Army, proposed to his fellow conspirators to use the reserve – or home army – for both the assassination and the ensuing coup.

Olbricht's plan, ironically, was based on original plans which had been designed by his staff and previously approved by Hitler himself for dealing with 'internal disturbances'. It was designed to combat a potential uprising by the millions of so-called foreign 'slave' workers. Under the code name 'Operation Valkyrie' the elements of the reserve army (trainees, soldiers on leave, training staff and cadres) would immediately unite and crush the internal disturbance.

Olbricht further developed the original 'Valkyrie' with two new instructions which ensured combat readiness of the reserve army and swift assembly of the units into battle groups.

The conspirators further adapted the 'Valkyrie plan' to suit their own aim of a coup d'état. The plan would kick into action once Hitler had been assassinated. The conspirators would then issue 'Operation Valkyrie' telegrams to all regional reserve army

[15] J Fest, op cit, p. 211.

commanders, informing them that the Führer had been killed by a treacherous group of party leaders who wanted to seize power. In order to restore the order in Germany and to avoid civil disturbances the army would declare martial law and take over power. In subsequent orders the conspirators would then order the regional commanders to arrest all Nazi party officials and SS commanders. The renegade German generals hoped that if they had the element of surprise on their side, the automatic chain of command would spring into action and ensure that the army could establish their power within 48 hours.

Once the army had seized power like this – almost through the backdoor – they would then try to petition the Western Allies again for peace. The renegade generals knew that Soviet Russia would never accept any peace feelers, but maybe Churchill and Roosevelt would change their minds.

The only potentially fatal flaw of the plan was that Hitler had expressly reserved the authority to implement the original 'Operation Valkyrie' for himself, with the commander of the reserve army, General Friedrich Fromm, authorized to give the

General Friedrich Olbricht (left) and General Friedrich Fromm.

cue only in an emergency. Therefore, the conspirators either had to win Fromm over, or set 'Valkyrie' in motion in his name. Olbricht was prepared to take Fromm into custody if necessary and sign the orders himself. But this risked questions of chain of command and delays might endanger the whole enterprise.

General Friedrich Fromm, born in 1888 into a Protestant family with strong military traditions, is a huge man, somewhat reserved in character, with strong beliefs in the army as the guarantor of Germany's status as a world-power. Fromm is no outright Hitler loyalist, but a fence-sitter who remains non-committal, keeping his options open, and back whichever comes out on top, the régime or the conspirators. Fromm's opportunism will be crucially decisive on the 20th July, 1944.

By summer 1943 – the military opposition against Hitler now had a strategy. But another assassination attempt in December 1943 equally failed because Hitler left a presentation of new uniforms prematurely. It became very clear that the opposition needed an assassin, someone who had courage, but also guaranteed direct and uninterrupted access to Hitler, in order to make the next assassination attempt successful.

On 10th August, 1943, a young lieutenant colonel was present at a dinner party at Colonel General Olbricht's house. Olbricht was told that this young man had confided in one of the fellow-conspirators, saying 'Since the generals have failed to do anything, it's now up to the colonels'. He had been badly injured during a British strafing attack while serving in the North African desert in April of that year. He had lost his right hand as well as the third and fourth fingers of his left, and he wore a black patch over his left eye. It was Claus von Stauffenberg.

> *I think having almost lost his life rather concentrated his thoughts. I think his superior motive was the moral aspect that the crimes had been committed in the name of Germany and he wanted this to be stopped. He was appalled by the way the war was managed, and how little resistance the leading generals were putting up against Hitler's decisions. Of course many of the elder officers had scruples about the oath and killing anybody including the head of state.*[16]

Stauffenberg was to imbue the military resistance with a vitality they had long been lacking. He sent an electric charge through the lifeless resistance networks as he quickly and naturally assumed a leadership role. He was familiar with all the complex religious, historical and traditional reasons that had stood in the way of action, but he had not lost sight of the basic truth that there were

[16] Interview Count Berthold von Stauffenberg, eldest son of Stauffenberg, 10/3/04.

limits for every soldier to loyalty and obedience. And that these limits had now been reached.

He had put aside all his scruples about treason and breaking the oath of allegiance to Hitler. He also dismissed all the foreign policy concerns of the other conspirators. He simply assumed that a government that had overthrown the Nazis would be able to negotiate with the Allies. Most importantly, Stauffenberg was determined to act against the dictator – at all cost – and that included sacrificing his own life. Stauffenberg's energy was infectious.

On 20th June, 1944, Stauffenberg assumed the duties as Chief of Staff to the Commander-in-Chief of the Reserve Army, General Friedrich Fromm. Stauffenberg was now in the key position to lead the coup.

As Stauffenberg boards the Heinkel 111 plane one month later to the day on the fateful 20th July 1944, the future of Germany and the course of the war hang in the balance. Will he be successful in assassinating Hitler, and will the army rebellion succeed in overthrowing the Nazi régime?

Von Stauffenberg and von Haeften arriving at the Wolf's Lair. (Reconstruction)

CHAPTER TWO

0830 Hours – London

Weapons of Mass Destruction

Everyone has his day and some days last longer than others.

Churchill, 1944

L ONDON, Thursday 20th July, 1944, the beginning of a hazy and grey British summer day. The city has changed its appearance under the threat from German bombs. Walls of sandbags cover the entrances to government buildings, anti-aircraft guns are positioned, and in order to protect the heart of the British government from invasion, St James's Park is criss-crossed with barbed wire fences and trenches. But this does not deter

A V1 'flying bomb' descending over the London skyline.

¹ Neil Cooke, interview, 9/02/2004.

Londoners from enjoying the park, even though it resembles more an obstacle course.[1]

Britain has now been at war with Nazi Germany for almost five years. And Londoners are recovering from yet another night of indiscriminate V1 bombs, Hitler's new vengeance weapon, unmanned jet propelled missiles which bring death and destruction to London and the South-East.

By the end of July 1944, the cumulative damage in London alone will reach 4640 killed, 13,571 seriously injured, 17,540 houses destroyed and 792,531 damaged, a third of which uninhabitable. London is again in the front line. The V1s are unleashed from launch sites in Nazi-occupied Northern Europe and first started when the Allies landed in Normandy six weeks ago, and haven't stopped since then. The vain hope of Londoners that after D-Day the war will now be fought only on the European Continent is shattered. Over half a million women and children are evacuated from London. Ironically, even the German PoWs incarcerated in Devizes in the South-East petition the House of Commons and ask to be evacuated to safer areas – without V1 bombings.

Prime Minister Churchill is in his bedroom in the No.10 Annexe, his wartime residence at Storey's Gate, Whitehall, just above the subterranean Cabinet War Rooms, and overlooking St James's Park. Churchill and his wife Clementine occupy very modest accommodations in the Annexe, which are actually small offices on the raised ground floor of the Ministry of Works. There is a bedroom for Mrs Churchill – and a bedroom for Mr Churchill, as well as a dining-room and a lounge. But there is no proper kitchen – all the food is cooked at the Downing Street residence and brought round to the Annexe by car with the saucepans wrapped in blankets.[2]

The Churchills moved into the No.10 Annexe when the traditional prime ministerial residence in Downing Street was deemed unsafe in October 1940 after bomb damage near-by. And as Churchill detested the subterranean Cabinet War Rooms, his wife and staff had to get accustomed to the often cumbersome and temporary accommodation of the No.10 Annexe. The location of the rooms is not ideal, as they are situated between the main door of the building and the offices of the PM's official staff. Because the threat exists of an attack on the Prime Minister's life by German agents, the men in charge of his security are manning machine-gun positions in the hallway leading to his private quarters.[3]

[2] Neil Cooke, interview, 9/02/2004.

[3] Elizabeth Layton, *Mr Churchill's Secretary*, London 1958, p-25-26.

Winston Churchill taking his breakfast in bed. (Reconstruction)

The war has not only taken its toll on the Downing Street building but also on Churchill himself, the oldest of the four wartime leaders. His personal physician, Lord Moran, has advised him to rest as much as he can between the meetings, briefings and statements in the Commons, which constitute Churchill's business of war.

It is 0830hours – and Winston Churchill is still in bed, which is not unusual. Churchill effectively runs the Second World War and the country from his bed, as one of his wartime secretaries, Elizabeth Nel, recalled in her memoirs after the war:

> *Mr Churchill would usually wake about 8 o'clock and would have breakfast in bed on a specially constructed tray which would fit around his belly. During this he would read through all the morning papers. He always noted when one was missing. Thereafter he lighted up his first cigar. He would recline in bed propped up with pillows, dressed in his favourite peacock dressing gown, which was green and gold with red dragons on it, and work on his Box, the key of which on*

a long silver chain, never left him. The Box was a rectangular black box which locked automatically on closing. There was a good number of these about. And 'Gimme my Box' was a phrase all his staff knew very well.[4]

Churchill working, as was his usual practice, from his bedroom. (Reconstruction)

Then at about 0900hours one of the secretaries on duty would enter the bedroom. They would be greeted by the heavy cigar smoke in his bedroom, and the grave look from the PM over his glasses, but no comment.

As Elizabeth Nel remembers, working for Churchill could be a daunting task:

The routine was that one would not wait to be summoned, but would quietly enter the room at 8.30am when one judged he had finished breakfast and reading the papers, sit at the silent typewriter, and having arranged everything in readiness for dictation, one would make oneself as much as part of the furniture as possible.[5]

Churchill was also very particular about his cigars.
Churchill's valet-butler at the time was one Frank Sawyers.

[4] E Layton, op. cit., p. 27-28.
[5] E Layton, op. cit., p. 49.

A V1 taking off from its launch pad.

Though still young he was hairless, short and round, pale of face and somewhat toothless. He was the custodian of the cigars. Churchill smoked between 8 to 10 a day. Indeed he never seemed to be happy for a moment without a cigar between his lips unless it was mealtimes. The cigar frequently went out and vast quantities of large-size matches were used and a certain amount of time consumed during the day to relighting them. They would burn along nicely at first, but then as their smoker's thoughts became fully engaged, their fire would die, and they would be used as a dummy, until their deficiency was noted and relighting performed.[6]

Lighting the first cigar of the day is a very special ritual:

> *Mr Churchill would like to light his first cigar of the day with a candle, and then woe betide the one who forgot and blew the candle out instead of carrying it from the room, as the waxy smell was not popular with Mr Churchill.*[7]

The mornings were often tense – especially during the

[6] E Layton, op. cit., p. 44-45.
[7] E Layton, op. cit., p. 50.

months of June and July 1944, when Churchill studied the overnight damage reports of the V1 bombing raids, and brought himself up to speed with the military situation in Normandy.

Churchill seen here at the Casablanca Conference with Foreign Secretary, Anthony Eden, on the far left. Field Marshal Sir Alan Brooke between them and Air Marshal Sir Arthur Teddar standing with pipe.

> *Frequently he was not in the best moods at this time of the day — perhaps from too little sleep. For some months I found these morning sessions with the Box a considerable strain, because as it often happened, his first appointment was only at luncheon. And one was closeted with him from 08.30am to 1 o'clock.*[8]

The Prime Minister found it more restful to work in bed, and would remain there during the morning, receiving visitors in his bedroom, and working the whole morning exclusively on his boxes. Half an hour was allowed for bathing and dressing, and the day would vary according to the business written on the

[8] E Layton, op. cit., p. 50.

'Card', a large white square with a space for each day of the month, on which all appointments were recorded.[9]

Churchill would take a nap after luncheon, which enabled him to work late into the night. The evenings were then filled with long official dinners with a considerable amount of alcohol. These evening briefings and meetings lasted often into the early hours, something which did not necessarily endear him to his staff, who did not have the luxury of snoozing in the afternoon, as Field Marshal Alan Brooke recorded in his diary:

> *At 10pm we had a frightful meeting with Winston which lasted till 2 am!! It was quite the worst we have had with him. He was tired as a result of his speech in the House concerning the flying bombs, he had tried to recuperate with drink. As a result he was in a maudlin, bad tempered, drunken mood, ready to take offence at anything, suspicious of everybody, and in a highly vindictive mood against the Americans. In*

London firemen tackling fires as a result of the bomb attacks.

[9] E Layton, op. cit., p.28.

Rescuing a Londoner that had been buried under rubble.

fact so vindictive that his whole outlook on strategy was warped. ...We withdrew at 2 am, having accomplished nothing beyond losing our tempers and valuable sleep![10]

Winston Churchill had a famously old fashioned way of expressing himself and this was entirely deliberate. He liked using Victorian expressions and these, together with other customs, became part of everyday work.

Very often Mr Churchill would use the word 'pray'. 'Pray let me have that report' or 'Pray see that there is no delay'. We called them 'Mr Churchill's prayers' because the memo would start with 'pray'. Our forces

The Home Secretary, Herbert Morrison (centre with glasses).

would often meet with 'a heavy prop', which was a stopping blow. 'The soft underbelly' was often mentioned, and the 'Herrenvolk' which was his term for the Nazis.[11]

Taking dictation from Churchill was a equally difficult task:

> *Churchill was in the habit of dictating straight on to the typewriter in order to save time, the war was pressing. It wasn't always easy to hear the PM. He had a slight speech impediment connected with the letter S. Then there was the cigar between his lips, and he usually paced up and down the room as he was dictating so that at times he was behind you and then again across the room. You had to be prepared to go fast in short bursts, to finish a sentence before the next started. All secretaries had to use noiseless typewriters, and when he finished dictating they had to hand over the Minute, letter or directive ready for signing, correct, unsmudged, complete. He would then sign or initial it, buzz for the Private Secretary and it would be dispatched, frequently topped with the bright red sign stating 'Action This Day'.[12]*

His daily routine helps Churchill to continue with the strenuous business of war against Nazi Germany. But by the 20th July, 1944 – the British PM has come under increasing pressure, at home and abroad.

[11] E Layton, op. cit., p.50.
[12] E Layton, op. cit., p 29, p 36-37.

Churchill was a small and energetic man. A heroic leader in public, but a volatile bully in private. He was notorious for his tendency to micro-manage and meddle in other people's business. Having never been to university he has a self-trained mind, and often approaches problems unscientifically.[13]

Goebbels, the German Propaganda Minister (centre) and Albert Speer, the Armaments Minister (right), watching the launch of rockets headed for London.

> *He does not know the situation, has a false picture of the distribution of forces and of their capabilities. A complete amateur of strategy, he swamps himself in details he should never look at and as a result fails ever to see a strategic problem in its true perspective.[14]*

But it was difficult to keep things in perspective in July 1944. Unlike his ally, Franklin D Roosevelt, who had never been exposed to nightly bombing raids, Churchill and London are the target again of German bombs, a devastatingly indiscriminate new weapon the flying bomb, the predecessor to today's scud and cruise missiles.

The German secret rocket weapons programme was known to the British government since April 1943. The danger was that these new weapons were believed to be inaccurate and therefore limited to a large target like London. Under the codename

[13] A Roberts, op. cit., p. 61-62.
[14] A Brooke, op. cit., 10th July 1944, p. 568.

'Operation Crossbow' intelligence on their development was collected, and the Ministry of Home Security was instructed to look into civil defence measures. Their estimates on casualties were based on a 2500kg German bomb which had fallen on Hendon on February 12th, 1941. No prior warning had been given by sirens. The blast demolished 19 houses, killed 85 people, hospitalized 148 and injured another 300. The Ministry estimated that a flying bomb would be able to kill 600 people and seriously injure a further 1200. The fear of rocket attacks in Whitehall however died down after D-Day.[15]

But then six days after the Normandy landings, on June 12th, 1944, the first flying bomb attacks on London started in earnest. In the first month some 2700 were launched at London with 1200 reaching the capital. On 27th June, Herbert Morrison, the Home Secretary, reported to Churchill and the War Cabinet that the V1s had killed 1600 people, seriously injured 4500 and damaged 200,000 homes. Civilian morale was deteriorating seriously. Between 30 to 40 tons of bombs were being dropped on London

A V1 rocket being 'rolled out' from an underground bunker to its launch pad.

[15] R Irons, *Hitler's Terror Weapons*, 2003, p. 70-71.

every day, and almost half of the RAF fighters were diverted in a futile battle to shoot down the flying bombs.[16]

The German V1s carried one ton of high explosives and travelled at a maximum speed of 400mph. They had a maximum flying distance of 200 miles, but the weather decreased this. A preset magnetic compass and gyroscopic auto-pilot determined and maintained its course.

These new German weapons were the first weapons of mass destruction. Hitler called them his miracle weapons (*Wunderwaffen*) but his propaganda chief Joseph Goebbels found the more appropriate term: *Vergeltungswaffen* – vengeance weapons, launched as retribution for the Allied aerial bombing raids.[17]

On July 18, 1944, a V1 rocket exploded in Lewisham High Street. Fifty-nine people were killed and over three hundred injured.

[16] R Lamb, *Churchill as war leader*, 1991, p.176
[17] Directive of J Goebbels to the German press June 16th 1944.

Churchill was more rattled by the flying bombs than by any other setback in the war and snapped at his colleagues. He felt the government had been napping and was exposed to heavy criticism from the public. On 6th July, 1944, he made two propositions: The first was that a hundred German towns with populations of between two to five thousand should be selected for total destruction by aerial bombardment. Ten were to be destroyed on the first night, the rest obliterated at the rate of one for every day that the flying bomb attacks continued.[18]

Churchill's second proposal was even more sensational: The PM was ready to authorize the use of poison gas if it could be shown that it was a matter of life and death for Britain or would shorten the war by a year.[19]

Churchill's suggestions horrified his military advisors. The first suggestion could endanger Allied PoWs inside Nazi Germany to become sitting targets. But with his second suggestion Churchill was contemplating to break all the fundamental conventions of war, as the use of poison gas was outlawed since 1925. The main concern of the chiefs was however the strategic inefficiency of poison gas. It also ignored the fact that only a few weeks earlier Churchill had told Montgomery that there was no question of using poison gas in the Normandy invasion, and Montgomery had ordered the British soldiers to leave their gasmasks behind.[20]

Sir Alan Brooke thought that it would be a diversion of the war effort – the flying bomb had already achieved this. Nearly 50% of the British air effort was already sucked up into combating the flying bombs, with some success. But it meant that these planes were not used for the advances in Normandy or for Allied bombings over Germany. Reprisal tactics like poison gas were in Alan Brooke's words 'a surrender of the initiative'. Furthermore, German morale had failed to break under the already heavy Allied air attacks on German cities. The Chiefs of Staff concluded that poison gas attacks would delay the advances of 'Operation Overlord' in Normandy and 'Operation Anvil' the invasion from the South of France. In particular, the chiefs felt that the initiation of poison gas warfare on the enemy would have an adverse effect on the morale of the British civilian population. The Chiefs recommended to review the situation at the beginning of August 1944.[21]

This was however not a satisfactory answer for the Prime

[18] R Lamb, op. cit., p. 308.
[19] R Irons, op. cit., p. 89.
[20] R Lamb, op. cit., p.308.
[21] R Irons, op. cit., p.89.

Minister, who replied the next day, on July 7th, to General
Ismay with a long memorandum – in circulation to every
member of the Chiefs of Staff Committee – and asking Ismay to
'think seriously about the use of poison gas':

*Churchill with Generals
Alan Brooke and Ismay.
(Reconstruction)*

> *It is absurd to consider morality on this topic when everybody used
> [gas] in the last war without a word of complaint from the moralists
> or the Church. In the last war the bombing of open cities was regarded
> as forbidden. Now everybody does it as a matter of course. It is simply
> a question of fashion changing as she does between long and short
> skirts for women. I want a cold-blooded calculation made as to how it
> would pay us to use poison gas, by which I principally mean mustard.
> …I should be prepared to do ANYTHING* [Churchill's capitals]
> *that would hit the enemy in a murderous place. I may certainly have
> to ask you to support me in using poison gas. We could drench the
> cities of the Ruhr and many other cities in Germany in such a way
> that most of the population would be requiring constant medical
> attention. I do not see why we should have all the disadvantages of*

*being the gentlemen while they have all the advantages of being the
cad …It may be several weeks or even months before I shall ask you
to drench Germany with poison gas and if we do it, let us do it 100
percent. In the meantime, I want the matter studied in cold blood by
sensible people and not by that particular set of psalm-singing
uniformed defeatists.*[22]

On the 8th July the Chiefs discussed Churchill's memorandum
– and referred the question of poison gas to the Vice Chiefs. But
Churchill wouldn't let go of the matter. Ten days later, on the 18th
of July, during his meeting with the Chiefs, Churchill asked again
to investigate the poison gas option as a means to retaliate against
the V1 attacks, and asked for 'a purely military examination' of the
probable effects of gas attacks.[23]

But while the Chiefs stall – it is Churchill who feels the pressure
from the public.

On 5th July the House demands that the PM explains before
them why the government hasn't been doing anything against the
flying bomb menace. This is followed by heated exchanges in the
House over the inadequacies of civil defence measures. Churchill
does make a statement the following day in the Commons on the
6th July.

But with continuing V1 bombardments, the government comes
again under attack the next day from London councillors who
demand that the deep shelters be opened and evacuation plans
for mothers and children put in place. The first deep shelter
opens on the 9th, and the second on the 13th, but the House
keeps criticising the PM.

The night of the 19th July, 1944, is one of the heaviest of V1
bombardments on London. Even Sir Alan Brooke is affected:

*19th July. A nasty disturbed night with about a dozen flying bombs in
the vicinity. The nearest landed about 150 yards away at about 3 am. It
displaced the window frame of our sitting room, and blew a lot of glass
out of the surrounding houses. I heard it coming, thought it was coming
unpleasantly close, so slipped out of bed and took cover behind my bed
on the floor to avoid glass splinters.*[24]

The next morning – on Thursday, 20th July, 1944 – Churchill
broods over the question whether poison gas warfare against
Germany would stop the flying bombs. He will again urge his
closest advisers Ismay and Alan Brooke to investigate his original
request from the beginning of the month. He will ask 'for a
dispassionate report on the military aspects of threatening to use

[22] Prime Minister's Personal Minute, serial No D.217/4
[23] PRO CAB 98/36, CBC(44) 7th meeting; and R Irons, op. cit., p. 90.
[24] A Brooke, op. cit., Diary entry 19th July 1944, p. 571.

poison gases on the enemy…' He now demands this report in three days.[25]

As Churchill reads the overnight V1 bombing reports on the 20th July 1944, and tallies up the casualties so far, one wonders whether a successful assassination of Adolf Hitler would alleviate the PM's main worry. Could the war in Europe end sooner rather than later?

[25] R Irons, op. cit., p. 90-91.

CHAPTER THREE

0900 Hours – Moscow

The Supreme War Lord

Blood for Blood.

Stalin, summer 1944

Moscow, 0900 hours, KGB Secret Object No. One. Marshal Stalin is sleeping on his divan in his dacha in Kuntsevo, six miles north-east of Moscow. As usual he has fallen asleep in the early hours of the morning after reading his history books, wearing all his clothes and boots.[1] The Soviet people believe their glorious leader lives and works in the Kremlin where the light can be seen burning twenty-four hours a day. A light in the Kremlin is indeed always burning, but just in front of a picture of Lenin. Stalin, however, runs the Soviet Empire and directs the Great War from his comfortable summer-villa.[2]

Valetchka – Stalin's housekeeper – wakes him. She is an always smiling, cheerful Russian peasant woman, simple and young. Valetchka looks after all Stalin's appetites. She cooks his meals, brings them in and serves him at the table. She is probably his part-time mistress too. Valetchka is resolutely unpolitical and uncomplicated, and devoted to Stalin. In all the years after his death, she never spilled a single one of his secrets.[3]

After a light breakfast, Stalin will spend most of the waking hours at work. He will read despatches, coded telegrams, operational plans and diplomatic correspondence. More than any of the other war leaders, Stalin truly dominates his nation's war effort. Hitler and his generals coexist in a constant state of tension. Churchill imposes his will by argument. Roosevelt largely presides over rather than direct his chiefs of staff. Stalin

[1] S S Montefiore, *Stalin. The Court of the Red Tsar*, p. 392.
[2] S S Montefiore, op. cit., p. 385.
[3] S S Montefiore, interview 14/03/04.

A reconstruction of Josef Stalin sitting at his desk.

dictates.[4]

Anything that Stalin utters is final and decisive, regardless of the way it is drafted, as he is the General Secretary of the Communist Party, master of the Politburo, Prime Minister of the Soviet Government, Head of the State, Commander-in-Chief of the Soviet Forces, and Chairman of the Soviet Defence Council. Once Stalin gives an order the whole system goes into action.[5]

He is a tireless, extraordinarily ruthless and incessant warlord. As supreme commander-in-chief of the Soviet armies and chairman of the state defence council he commands every detail of the war. He commands the armies, but also decides what tobacco the soldiers smoke and what pamphlets they read.[6]

All information flows to him – day and night. He holds situation conferences at noon and late at night. Three telephones dominate his desk, which he uses almost like weapons, calling his generals at the front line, phoning soldiers and officers, calling his ministers late at night, telling them what to do, down to the smallest detail. Famously, he is capable of threatening and be charming at the

[4] J Keegan, *The Second World War*, p. 380.

[5] D Volkogonov, *Stalin Triumph and Tragedy*, p. 451.

[6] S S Montefiore, interview 14/03/04.

same time. He will ask whether everything is alright at the front, but then finish an order with the short reprimand 'fail this and we'll make you shorter by a head'.[7]

Stalin rules the lives of his generals, personally decreeing their rota of work and rest. In the case of Army General Alexander Vasilevsky, Stalin orders that he sleep from 4am to 10am without fail. He sometimes rings Vasilevsky like a strict nanny to check that he is asleep. If he answers the phone, Stalin curses him. Yet, Vasilevsky finds it impossible to attend Stalin's nocturnal dinners and then do all his work, so he has to break the rules, stationing an adjutant by his phone to reply: 'Comrade Vasilevsky's resting until 10.'[8]

Stalin expects to receive bulletins from his roving military liaison officers, either by phone or in person, three times a day, in the morning, at noon and late at night. And he rebukes them if

A propaganda picture of Josef Stalin during the war years.

[7] S S Montefiore, interview 14/03/04.
[8] S S Montefiore, op. cit., p. 392.

they are late. The long nights are spent dictating orders directly
to the officers of his General Staff between midnight and three or
four in the morning.[9]

*Another wartime portrait
of Josef Stalin.*

In the evenings, Stalin would often drive in his convoy of
speeding Packards from the dacha back to the Kremlin, and
have further meetings. His appointment's book for 19th July,
1944, shows that his meetings started at 2225pm and lasted
until 0045am, by which time he left the Kremlin and drove back
to the dacha.[10]

Stalin's only form of relaxation seems to be his nocturnal
dinners at the dacha. Having no personal friends or family
members living with him, he dines almost always with the same
inner group of fellow comrades with whom he runs the country
and the war, Molotov – in charge of foreign relations, Beria – in
charge of intelligence and war production, and Malenkov – in
charge of aircraft production. Much of their talk is shop:

> *Everyone helped themselves from heavy silver dishes and sat where
> they liked. These dinners lasted from 10 at night till 4 or 5 in the
> morning with conversations ranging from anecdotes to serious*

[9] D Volkogonov, op. cit., p. 464-467.
[10] Stalin's Appointments Book 1924-1953, 4, 1996, p. 66.

Nikita Krushchev (left) and General Alexander Vasilevsky

political and philosophical subjects.[11]

And there is a great deal of food buffet-style: fish, cabbage soup, various meat dishes, bread, spices, vegetables and mushrooms, and bottles of dry wine, vodka and brandy:[12]

> *Stalin ate food quantities that would have been enormous even for a much larger man. He usually chose meat, which was a sign of his mountain origins. He also liked all kinds of local specialities in which this land of various climes and civilisations abounded. He drank more moderately than the others, usually mixing red wine and vodka in little glasses. I never noticed any signs of drunkenness in him, whereas I could not say the same for Molotov, let alone Beria who was a drunkard.*[13]

Nikita Krushchev later recalled these dinners as a waste of time:

> *I don't think there has ever been a leader of comparable responsibilities who wasted more time than Stalin did just sitting around the dinner table eating and drinking.*[14]

At the end of the day, Stalin always set some time aside to review

[11] M Djilas, *Conversations with Stalin, reflecting on June 1944*, p. 163.

[12] J Ellis, *One day in a very long war*, p. 15.

[13] M Djilas, op. cit., p. 163.

[14] N Krushchev, *Krushchev Remembers*, p. 78.

the latest Soviet news reels and films. The dinner party would move to the cinema room, and watch them together. On the rare occasions when Stalin is alone, he prefers to listen to music from phonograph records. Of the new records delivered to him, he tries out the greater part himself, and immediately rates them. Each record is labelled in his own hand as 'good', 'tolerable', 'bad', or 'trash'. Only records bearing the first two labels are left next to a Soviet-made phonograph with a crank. And Stalin would carry it himself to where ever he wanted to listen to it.[15]

Stalin – now sixty-four years old - is small in stature but of powerful physique. Still the war has taken its toll on him.

He was of very small stature and ungainly built. His torso was short and narrow, while his legs and arms were too long. His left arm and

Josef Stalin, Franklin D Roosevelt and Winston Churchill at the Teheran Conference in 1943. Behind Stalin stands Molotov, the Soviet Foreign Minister, and the tall figure of Anthony Eden, the British Foreign Minister, between Churchill and Roosevelt.

[15] S M Shtemenko, *The Soviet General Staff at War 1941-1945*, p. 267.

Adolf Hitler and his press secretary Gruppenführer-SS Otto Dietrich.

Franklin D Roosevelt in 1942.

Hitler with Field Marshal Wilhelm Keitel and General Alfred Jodl.

Hitler with his Alsation 'Blondi'.

Hitler with (l to r) Martin Bormann, Heinrich Himmler and Wilhelm Keitel.

FDR with his service chiefs.

Winston S. Churchill.

Reichsmarschall Hermann Göring talking to Hitler.

Adolf Hitler at the Wolf's Lair after the bomb plot.

An early photograph of the Italian dictator Benito Mussolini,

Londoners salvaging what they can after V1 raids.

Churchill, in the uniform of an RAF Air Commodore, shakes hands with Stalin.

shoulder seemed rather stiff. He had quite a paunch and his hair was sparse. His face was white, with ruddy cheeks, the coloration characteristic of those who sit in offices too long, known as the 'Kremlin complexion'. His teeth were black and irregular, turned inwards. Not even his moustache was thick and firm. Still the head was not a bad one; it had something of the common people about it – with those yellow eyes and a mixture of sternness and mischief.[16]

Stalin has a quick intelligence and a phenomenal memory but little formal education. His father was a boot-maker and his mother took in washing. Stalin is a man of enormous self-confidence and single-mindedness.

I was also surprised by his accent. One could tell that he was not a Russian. He spoke with a heavy Georgian accent, but his Russian vocabulary was rich and his manner of expression vivid and flexible, full of Russian proverbs and sayings.[17]

He is a modest man, taking care of everything himself, writing his speeches himself and answering all his mail by hand.

One thing did surprise me, Stalin had a sense of humour – a rough humour, self-assured, but not entirely without subtlety and depth. His reactions were quick and acute – and conclusive, which did not mean that he did not hear the speaker out, but it was evident that he was no

[16] M Djilas, op. cit., p. 156.
[17] Ibid.

friend of long explanations.[18]

Soviet mobile rocket launchers at the start of Operation Bagration in July 1944.

Like Churchill, Stalin has no personal vanity, wearing a simple grey military coat and soft boots. Like Churchill – he loves his tobacco. And like Roosevelt, Stalin is a chain smoker. He prefers American cigarettes to Russian, which he holds between his thumb and index finger and puffs with his chin in the palm of his hand.[19]

The Big Three – Stalin, Churchill and Roosevelt – had only met the year before in Teheran for the first time. It had been a guarded affair. Stalin recognised in Roosevelt a fellow-pragmatist but he believed that Churchill was as much anti-Communist, as he was anti-Nazi. He admired Churchill's bullish strength, but distrusted him. The feeling was mutual. The glue between the three disparate Allies is their fight against Hitler. Once this glue will disappear, the cracks will open in this uneasy Alliance.

Stalin's famous quip in June 1944 summed up his feelings for his two Allies:

> *Churchill is the kind of man who will pick your pocket for a kopek, if you don't watch him. Yes, pick your pocket for a kopek! By God, pick your pocket for a kopek. Roosevelt is not like that. He dips his hand for bigger coins. But Churchill, will do it for a kopek.*[20]

[18] Ibid.
[19] R Edmonds, *The Big Three*, p. 85.
[20] M Djilas, op. cit., p 163.

The first two years of the Second World War have been an unmitigated disaster for the Soviet Union, made worse by Stalin's bungling. Soviet losses in human life have been extraordinary. By the end of the war the blood letting of the Soviet people – civilians and soldiers – will amount to around 26 million people. And yet these losses are sustainable by the Soviet Union in a way that would be impossible with the Western Allies.[21]

But since the victory in Stalingrad, the Supreme Commander

Soviet troops erecting a new frontier post after reclaiming territory from the German forces during Operation Bagration.

[21] J Keegan, op. cit., p. 379.

realises that the tide is turning in the war against the German
invaders. At Teheran in November 1943 he assures Roosevelt and
Churchill that he will support the D-Day invasion with the launch
of a massive offensive against the German armies at the Eastern
Front. The date Stalin chooses is the third anniversary of Hitler's
invasion of the Soviet Union: 'Operation Bagration' begins on
Friday, 23rd June, 1944, on the fields of Byelorussia and lasts 67
days and nights.

Soviet troops during
Operation Bagration.

No previous strike by the Red Army has been prepared more
carefully. The ultimate aim of Operation Bagration is to open
the road to Berlin. It is one of the largest offensive operations
in the Second World War and totally changes the strategic
situation along the Eastern Front. The operation is named after
Pyotr Bagration, a Georgian general who died a heroic death
against the invasion army of Napoleon Bonaparte in 1812.
Everything about this offensive is overwhelming and full of

A Soviet officer checks ammunition, left by retreating German forces, to see if it is reusable.

symbolism.[22]

To defend the Byelorussian salient, the German High Command has 63 divisions, three infantry brigades, totalling 1,200,000 men. They are equipped with 900 tanks and assault guns, plus 9,500 field guns and mortars. They have 1,350 combat aircraft at their disposal. On battle alert for Stalin are 2,400,000 men 36,000 guns and mortars, 5,200 tanks, and 5,300 combat aircraft. Stalin is throwing three cavalry corps – Bagration sees the last major cavalry attack of the Second World War, and perhaps of all time – twenty infantry armies, two tank armies, five air armies and twelve tank corps at the German Wehrmacht.[23]

[22] J Keegan, op. cit., p. 402.
[23] A Axell, *Stalin's war through the eyes of his commanders*, p. 99-100.

At exactly 0600 hours we heard the roar of the first salvo of Katyusha rocket-launchers. The air trembled. More than 1,800 guns and mortars launched a hail of fire at the enemy's defences. Our softening-up bombardment kept the following pattern: a five minute attack by all our artillery, a 30-minute pause. Then aimed fire for 85 minutes to destroy enemy covered positions, to be followed by 20 minutes of direct fire to destroy enemy gun emplacements, and finally 40 minutes of fire to neutralise defences in the forward line and

immediately behind it in the sector earmarked for penetration and in adjacent areas. To avoid a pause between the end of the bombardment and the start of the attack our batteries began gradually to shift their fire, without diminishing its intensity, only three minutes before the infantry and tanks rushed the enemy positions. This enabled the units carrying out the attack to follow the fire barrage 75 to 100 yards behind the shell bursts.[24]

German troops on order from Hitler to fight to the last man, stubbornly resist. Counter-attacks follow one after another. Bloody battles take place. Positions change hands repeatedly. Some German positions are completely taken by surprise. Russian forces advance in some areas far further than originally planned. Overall German resistance is broken and defences are broken swiftly. The Red Army encircle their positions and destroy them. Byelorussia suffers untold damage. Along the route of German soldiers retreating, Russian soldiers see only chimneys standing among the ruins – and gallows from which local citizens are strung up.[25]

By 5th July, 1944, the main elements of the German 4th Army are cut off and more than 105,000 men encircled. Some generals order their men to stop fighting:[26]

Our situation is hopeless. Our best avenues of escape have been cut off. Our units are scattered and in disorder. A tremendous number of wounded were left behind. Therefore I order an immediate end to all resistance.[27]

When Bagration ends Hitler has lost more than 1,000,000 men, and the German army has lost one third of its total strength. The Eastern Front has collapsed, and the road is paved for the Battle for Berlin. For the first time in the war, the territory of the German Reich itself is now under threat from the advances of the Red Army.[28]

Stalin celebrates the battle on 17th July, 1944, by showing off the first spoils of his victory: 57,000 German prisoners of war are marched through the stunned and silent crowds along the streets of Moscow. They include 18 generals and 1,200 officers. The prisoners have been transported from the Byelorussian front in 28 special trains to Moscow. The procession sets off at 9am and ends at 4pm. The next morning the German prisoners are transported to the camps in the East.[29]

[24] General Kuzma Galitsky eye-witness report.
[25] A Axell, op. cit., p. 102.
[26] A Axell, op. cit., p.103.
[27] General Friedrich Wilhelm Muller, commander of 12th Army Corps.
[28] J Keegan, op. cit., p. 403.
[29] D Volkogonov, op. cit., p. 476-477.

It is now clear that Stalin has broken the German army's might in the East and is the undisputed supreme warlord of the summer of 1944. He can now begin again to consider how he and the Soviet Union can best profit geopolitically from the war's concluding stage.

As Stalin rises on this morning of 20th of July, 1944, the war is going well for him. His troops have Nazi-occupied Poland firmly in their sight, and Berlin will soon be in his grasp. If Hitler was assassinated today, and the German Army would plead conditional surrender, the advances of the Red Army might be halted. This would scupper all his well-laid out plans.

CHAPTER FOUR

0900 Hours – 1000 Hours Rastenburg

Inside the Wolf's Lair

We must turn the newly won Eastern territories into a Garden of Eden.

Adolf Hitler

THE Wolf's Lair, Hitlers secret Field Headquarters in the East, located near the small town of Rastenburg in German-occupied Poland.

An intricate network of wooden huts and barracks, and concrete bunkers, covering nearly three square kilometres, hidden deep in an extensive forest surrounded by swamps. It is Hitlers largest headquarters. It took over 2000 workers and over two years to construct and enforce the around 80 buildings that make up the Lair. The compound is almost a complete town in itself, and boasts two military airfields, a power station, a railway station, air purification installations for the raised ground bunkers, and water and supply drainage system, and an extensive communications network.[1]

More than two thousand people make up the Wolf's Lair population: around 300 senior officers, generals and field marshals, 1200 ordinary soldiers, 150 security guards of the SS, and 300 administrative personnel, like secretaries, drivers, telephonists, barbers, waiters and cooks. The Lair has a cinema, a barber shop, a sauna, and a casino.[2]

The whole complex is protected by a high-security system of checkpoints, walls, barbed wire, booby traps and mines. The prevailing atmosphere is gloom and monotony. Visitors describe the place as a blend between monastery and concentration camp. Italian Foreign Minister Ciano, once compared the inhabitants of the Wolf's Lair with troglodytes, and found the atmosphere depressing. The small unadorned rooms are in striking contrast to the palatial grandeur and theatrical lavishness Hitler enjoys at his

[1] U Neumaerker/R Conrad/C Woywodt, *Wolfsschanze*, p. 53-63.
[2] U Neumaerker et al, op. cit., p. 71.

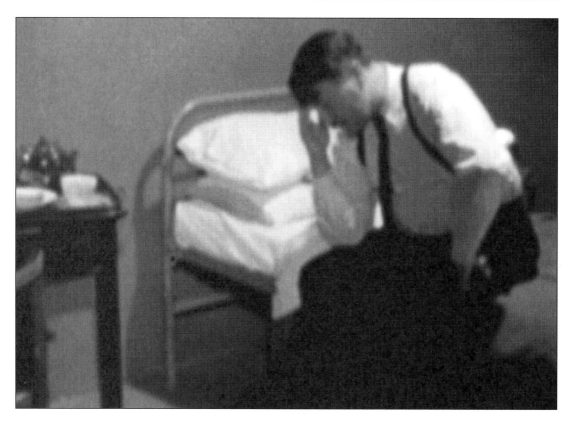

mountain retreat, the Berghof, or in the Reichs-Chancellery in Berlin.[3]

Hitler spent 800 days at the Wolf's Lair and hated every one of them. During the winter months, the Wolfs Lair was icy and even though a special heating system was installed, none of the wooden barracks or concrete bunkers ever got really comfortably warm. During the hot summer months, the place was invested by mosquitoes, and unbearably humid.[4] The summer of 1944 was extremely hot, and even the security guards in their huts had to be equipped with mosquito nets around their helmets.[5] Everybody suffered under the extreme heat, and was relieved when in May 1944 Hitler ordered that the German High Command was temporarily transferred to the Berghof. But the worsening situation of the war in the East meant, that Hitler and his staff had to leave the Berghof on the 14th of July and return to the grim cave world of the Wolf's Lair. Hitler would never return to his beloved Alpine retreat.[6]

It is Thursday, 20th July, 1944, another sultry summer day. In

Adolf Hitler in his sparse bedroom in the Wolf's Lair, having just dressed. (Reconstruction)

[3] C Puciato, *Wolfsschanze*, p. 35.
[4] J Fest, Hitler, *Eine Karriere*, p. 667.
[5] T Junge, *Bis zur letzten Stunde*, p. 140-142.
[6] C Schroeder, *Er war mein Boss*, p. 146.

the chill of his concrete bunker, Adolf Hitler rises. He is 5 foot 9 tall, but in the later years of the war walks with a slight stoop due to his scoliosis. He is also slightly overweight.[7]

Like Stalin and Churchill he adheres to a very strict and, in Hitlers case, a particularly gruelling daily régime.

At precisely 10am Hitler's valet, Heinz Linge, knocks on the Führers door. *SS-Obersturmbannführer* Heinz Linge has been in Hitler's service since 1933 and his head valet since 1939. He is,

Heinz Linge, Hitler's valet, seen here with the rank of Sturmbannführer-SS.

[7] M Hauner, Hitler. *A Chronology of his Life and Time*, 1983, p. 191.

Reconstruction of Hitler's valet, Heinz Linge bringing a breakfast tray.

however, much more than a valet. He is a butler, a personal assistant, a confidante, a master of ceremonies. Even the highest ranking generals first ask Linge 'What's Hitlers mood today?', or 'When is a good time to speak to the Führer?' Linge knows how to interpret Hitler's moods. Hitler totally trusts and confides in him. Linge is the only person, besides his doctors, who handles Hitler's medication.[8]

After knocking on the door, Linge tells him the exact time and delivers a simple breakfast with a herbal tea infusion and the overnight news bulletins. In July 1944, Linge also delivers the overnight success reports on the V1 bomb raids. Hitler will already be dressed. He will be wearing black trousers, a white shirt and a black tie.[9]

Unlike, Churchill, who doesn't mind, or Roosevelt, who needs assistance dressing, Hitler detests it when people see him half-naked. He insists on dressing and undressing himself on his own. Only at the end of the year, when he will be too ill to rise from his bed, will his staff for the first time see him in a night-gown, and

[8] T Junge, op. cit., p. 45.
[9] T Junge, op. cit., p. 45.

Hitler with Josef 'Sepp' Dietrich, Eva Braun and his dog, Blondi.

their Führer in bed. This insistence on keeping up appearances is all part of Hitlers acute awareness for image branding and mystique.[10]

Ever since the war began, Hitler resorted to a very simple soldiers dress: He wears a field-grey tunic with crossed over fastening, on which he only wore the World War One Iron Cross 1st Class. His generals are all covered in medals and decorations, but the Führer's modest dress set him apart all the more.[11]

[10] J Fest, op. cit., p. 668.
[11] J Fest, interview 10/03/03, London.

Equally plain as his dress is Hitler's accommodation. He prefers an austere, almost soldier-like lifestyle. He sleeps on a standard German army field bed, and has no personal effects with him, except for a photograph of his mother on his bedside-table. All part of the self-imposed sacrifice he insists upon.[12]

Hitler's secretaries; (above) Christa Schroeder and Gerda 'Dara' Christian. (Right) Gertrud 'Traudl' Junge.

After breakfast Hitler walks his Alsation 'Blondi' on a tiny piece of land adjacent to his bunker. Its one of the Führer's pastimes to teach the dog new tricks and show her off to his staff.[13]

Hitlers obsession with neatness and cleanliness is practically clinical. If he has patted Blondi, he will never shake hands with anyone without going to wash his hands first.[14]

Hitler spends most of the morning cooped up in his bunker, brooding over reports, and dictating to his secretaries, Christa Schroeder or Traudl Junge. Both women welcome being called in for dictation, as this means temporary refuge from the sweltering heat. The Führer liked to work in very low temperatures. Traudl Junge later recalled that the generals always came out of briefings with red noses and blue hands.[15]

Then at one o'clock, he will summon his High Command for

[12] Ibid.
[13] Ibid.
[14] T Junge, op. cit., p. 43.
[15] T Junge, op. cit., p. 44.

*Dr Theodor Morell,
Hitler's personal
physician.*

the lunchtime situation briefing. After which Hitler will lunch with his advisors and staff. The meals at the Führer's table are notorious for their blandness and simplicity.

After lunch, more conferences, dictation, receptions of guests until the evening situation briefing, this takes place during the night.[16]

All the reports show that by the summer 1944, Hitler is overcome by melancholic moods and he suffers greatly from sleeplessness. When midnight approaches, his inner circle is invited to join the Führer for some cake and discussion. Secretaries and adjutants try desperately to force their eyes open as Hitler discharges his inner tensions in nocturnal tirades and monologues until the greying dawn, when he finally retreats to his bedroom and lies down for a brief slumber, he will be awoken at nine o'clock by the scrubwomen, pushing their brooms against his bedroom door.[17]

[16] T Junge, op. cit. p. 45.
[17] T Junge, op. cit. p. 138.

The torture of this daily schedule can only be kept up with the help of Hitler's personal physician. Dr Theodore Morell, whose medication and drug-like preparations enable Hitler to meet the strain he puts on his body.

Morell gives Hitler daily injections shortly after breakfast: sulphanilamide, glandular preparations, glucose, or hormones that are supposed to improve or regenerate his circulation, Hitlers intestinal flora, or the state of his nerves, all in all 90 different concoctions. Hitler's inner circle sarcastically call Morell the Reichs Injection Minister.[18]

As with any other drug addict, the dealer has to increase the doses, and shorten the intervals between injections to maintain the performance of the drugs. Morell's drugs replace the euphoria Hitler received during his public speaking. Living like a virtual recluse, Morell's drugs are the only recharge for Hitler. But on top of these stimulants, Morell has to administer sedatives to calm Hitlers jangled nerves. The result of this constant interference

Hitler, younger than either Stalin, Roosevelt or Churchill, in the latter war years looked increasingly aged. In 1944 Hitler was just 55 years of age.

[18] J Fest, op. cit., p. 669.

with his body – at times Hitler takes up to 28 different drugs – becomes evident in the summer of 1944.[19]

At 55 years old, Hitler is the youngest of the four war leaders, and yet he is old and worn out before his time. His hair is rapidly greying and he walks with a pronounced stoop, mostly with a cane, hesitantly. He has difficulty co-ordinating his movements and he can no longer endure bright light – for this reason his field cap is fitted with a greatly enlarged visor. Finally, he suffers from Parkinson's syndrome, which shows in the trembling of his left hand.[20] One member of his medical staff observed that Dr Morell's treatment was drawing the life out of rather Hitler than improving it. It seemed as if Hitler aged every year not a year, but four or five years.[21]

The overnight reports Hitler studies on the morning of this 20th July, 1944, hold no good news for him.

The summer of 1944 is a time of desperate crisis for Hitler. The war seems to turn against him and all fronts seem to be wavering. East Prussia and Silesia are under threat from the advancing Red Army. France might be lost as the Allied invasion forces make headway from Normandy. Nazi Germany's old ally, Fascist Italy, is in dire straits. Is it still worthwhile to raise support and troops for Mussolini's crumbling Northern Italian Fascist Republic, when the Allies are advancing from the South of Italy? The most burning issue is however the faltering Eastern front and the successful advances of the Red Army into German-occupied Poland. On the 20th July the frontline is a mere 150km away from Hitlers Headquarters.

At the beginning of the Second World War Hitler inspired his High Command and he was brilliant in offensive situations when he suddenly attacked and overran the enemy. But in defensive situations he has a shocking lack of imagination. And it is this lack of strategy which leads to the enormous German casualties in the campaign against the Soviet Union. Hundred of thousands of soldiers are needlessly sacrificed in Stalingrad at the end of 1942. Their deaths were a direct result of Hitlers lack of strategic imagination: for him there was no retreat or giving up of positions. In Hitler's thinking based on the belief that will-power will triumph and bring victory, fighting to the end will force success.[22]

When on 22nd June, 1944, three years to the day after Hitler

---

[19] J Fest, op. cit., p.672.

[20] On Hitlers drug addiction see I Kershaw, *Hitler 1936-1945. Nemesis*, p. 612; J Fest, op. cit., p. 672; D Irving, *The Secret Diary of Hitlers Doctor*, p. 113.

[21] J Fest, interview 10/03/04.

[22] Professor Karl Brandt, quoted in J Fest, op. cit., p.673

In the East the defeated Wehrmacht troops were rounded up in thousands by the increasingly victorious Soviet forces.

invaded the Soviet Union – Stalin launches the massive summer offensive Operation Bagration, Hitlers order is, fortified places are to be held at all costs, every square metre of land is to be defended. The consequences are predictable: the Red Army sweeps around the strongholds and encircles the German divisions, wears them down and finally destroys them mercilessly. By mid-July 1944, Germany has lost 28 divisions with 350,000

*Reichsführer-SS
Heinrich Himmler*

men in a catastrophe even greater than Stalingrad. Hitler's response is characteristic: he sacks his commanders.[23]

As the blood-letting continues at the Eastern Front Hitler indulges in the propaganda success of the V1 bombs. He succeeds in his aim to sow terror and destruction in retaliation for the Allied bombing raids on Germany. What Germany however needs, in July 1944, is a decisive reversal of the military situation: she needs to stop the Allied bombers altogether, to crush the Allied landings in France, and then to swing the divisions East to defeat the Soviet Army. But Germany's forces are heavily overstretched and the V1 and the follow-up V2 are a very expensive weapon which doesn't solve any of these strategic dilemmas.

The grim reality in July 1944 is, that Germany is running short of explosives. Flak ammunition runs so short that flak gunners are ordered not to fire at aircraft unless they are directly attacking the installation they are supposed to protect. The 36,000 tons of

[23] J Fest, interview 10/03/04.

explosives used in the V1 and V2 together represents the total production of explosives in Germany between September to November 1944. Furthermore, Germany is critically short of fuel. The 11,000 tons of petrol to launch the 20,000 flying bombs are missing at the Eastern Front, where 1,500 tanks are immobilised for lack of fuel. Some commanders resort to blowing up their tanks, because they have no fuel to move them.[24] In military terms the V1 is a total failure. They are inaccurate, use vast amounts of resources, badly needed at the Eastern front, and are incredibly expensive to make.

Hitler's world is beginning to crash, and the reasons for his discontent are manifold. His secretary, Christa Schroeder, remembers that on 18th July, during lunch in his bunker, Hitler is clearly ill at ease. He reveals to her that he has a foreboding that something might happen to him. He has an inkling that someone wants to assassinate him, and exclaims, 'Nothing must happen to me now, because there is nobody who could take over.'[25]

Hitler's personal security is in the hands of the SS. Heinrich Himmler discussed the possibility of a paratrooper attack on the Wolf's Lair with the Führer on 15th July, 1944, and an entire battalion was concealed in the woods with tanks and anti-aircraft guns.[26]

At 1145am Dr Morell visits Hitler to give him his usual injection and administer a cocaine-adrenaline solution in the form of eye-drops. Apparently, the Führer suffers from influenza and conjunctivitis in both eyes. Shampoo got into his left eye, smarting badly.[27] After the lunch, Hitler expects Benito Mussolini to arrive at the Wolf's Lairs train station. For political reasons Hitler earlier conceded to him the right to raise four new divisions to fight back against the Allied advances in Italy. On consideration, Hitler is undecided whether to go ahead with it. The meeting will be a difficult one. Mussolini is due at 1430hours.[28] Hitler instructs his staff to bring the daily one o'clock situation briefing forward by half an hour, to accommodate the Duce's visit, – a minor alteration in Hitler's schedule, but one that will have enormous consequences for Count von Stauffenberg, who on this day is flying to the Wolf's Lair to kill him.

As Hitler attends to his reports, it seems that the 20th July will be just another long day of bad news from the Eastern Front.

---

[24] I Kershaw, op. cit., p. 647.
[25] R Irons, *Hitlers Terror Weapons*, p. 166.
[26] C Schroeder, op. cit., p. 148.
[27] P Hoffmann, *Hitlers Personal Security*, p. 242.
[28] D Irving, op. cit., p. 115.

CHAPTER FIVE

1100 Hours – San Diego
The Dying President

I felt thrilled sitting on a hill in an automobile, watching the bug-like approach of the landing crafts ...and the thousands of small figures breaching the surf, running up to the beach.

Roosevelt 20th July, 1944.

OCEANSIDE Naval Base, 40 miles north of San Diego, California. President Franklin D Roosevelt observes an amphibious landing exercise conducted by the Fifth Marine Division from a vantage point atop a high bluff, overlooking miles of beach. He is confined to the comfort of his car. His Scotch terrier Fala, and his son Colonel James – Jimmy – Roosevelt are by his side.[1]

Five thousand marines and 3,000 naval personnel are employed in this practice invasion which constitutes their graduation test for the Fifth Marine Division after three months of intensive training. It is a colossal exercise, and the President later recalls how thrilled he was witnessing the shore bombardment by cruisers and destroyers.[2]

Roosevelt never really got close to active fighting. He found himself in some risky situations, particularly long distance high-altitude flights in un-pressurised planes, but the landing exercise he witnesses on the 20th July, 1944, is about as close as he ever got to the fighting. The Marines he watches will soon be heading out to fight the bloody battles of the Pacific, for real.[3]

Thursday, 20th July, 1944, is an unseasonably grey summer's day with low visibility.

The President is now in his 3rd term of office – and will today

---

[1] FDR Day by Day - The Pare Lorentz Chronology, Grace Tully's Appointment Diary for details on the day.
[2] J Bishop, *FDR's Last Year*, p. 110.
[3] W F Kimball, interview 16/03/04.

An increasingly ill-looking Franklin D Roosevelt.

be nominated for a record fourth term, a first and last in American history. 1944 will be his last full year in office. The American people – and as some historians believe – also the President himself are unaware how terminally ill he is. But today in San Diego he will receive a cruel reminder of his own frailty.[4]

Roosevelt is by far the most enigmatic of the four war leaders.

He has been able to remain detached from the business of war, an activity alien to his temperament. Such an aloofness is not granted to any of the other war leaders. Churchill revels in high command and dedicates his days and nights to war-making. Hitler has turned himself into a military hermit. Stalin's wartime routine conforms strangely to Hitler's: secretive, nocturnal and

[4] R Ferrell, *The Dying President*, p. 15.

FDR being examined by his doctor. (Reconstruction)

troglodyte.

But Roosevelt scarcely alters his pattern of life after Pearl Harbor. Unthreatened by air-attacks, he continues to live in the White House, occasionally vacationing at Hyde Park. He sees nothing of the war at first hand, no bombed out cities, no troops at the front, no prisoners, no after-effects of battle, and probably he does not choose to.[5]

In stark contrast to the three other leaders who usually meddle or contradict their military advisors, Roosevelt listens to his generals, and most always does what they recommend, but equally has no qualms about reversing them.[6]

He pursues a timetable which drives the purposeful and methodical on his staff to despair. He begins his working day not before ten in the morning, takes few calls at night, and travels little. His mobility is of course limited by his physical disability, which is the result of polio he contracted in 1921. It has left his legs paralyzed and FDR needs help for every daily routine activity. Any other person would have crumbled under this total dependency on others in the most private and personal moments. But Roosevelt's response to his crippling disease is inner strength, which adds to his breezy, optimistic style, and makes him a formidable persona.[7]

Roosevelt refuses to let his paralysis affect his job. He ignores

[5] J Keegan, *The Second World War*, p. 458.
[6] W F Kimball, interview 16/03/04.
[7] W F Kimball, *Forged in War*, p. 4.

it. He is in charge, not the disability and he does everything possible to cover it up. When talking to people he will be seated in an ordinary chair. When giving a speech he arranges to have his wheelchair pushed to the ramp surrounded by Secret Service men until he is on the podium and can lock in his braces and an assistant can pull him up erect. If possible he will speak from an automobile. His disability is never publicly acknowledged and is kept secret with the help of a co-operative press corps (something that is unthinkable today), but also by very vigilant Secret Service men who confiscate films that might show it. In the Roosevelt Library collection of 35,000 still photographs, until quite recently, only two show the President in a wheelchair, and no newsreels show him lifted, carried or pushed. Many of his fellow Americans really did not know that their President is incapable of walking unaided.[8]

Roosevelt's leadership-style – coloured by his physical infirmity and the secret he is keeping from the people – is to be

Reconstruction of FDR travelling on his personal train, the 'Ferdinand Magellan'.

[8] HG Gallagher, *FDR's Splendid Deception*, p. 34.

The President's wife, Eleanor Roosevelt.

in sole control and to limit the power of any individual who works with him. On the surface it might appear as a chaotic administrative style, but it works for him and he is undoubtedly a highly effective administrator.

Roosevelt maintains control by a number of stratagems. He often will put two different people on the edges of the same job, without telling them, only for them to find out that they have been pitted against each other by him. The one who does the best job will end up in charge, while the other one resigns in frustration. FDR seems to delight in being the 'only person who knew everything about a project', he seems to obtain a sense of power, which he loves.

Government under Roosevelt is so personal, that only the nation's chief executive knows how it works. Ultimately, his successor, Harry S Truman, will need tutelage on how to deal with the different constituencies. Roosevelt has created a Rubic Cube – and only he knows the operating instructions.[9]

The President is not afraid to fire people, but to give two people the same task is his way of working out the best solution to a problem, and who is the best man to do the job.[10] Roosevelt's

[9] R Ferrell, op. cit., p. 151.
[10] W F Kimball, op. cit., p. 35. and interview 16/03/04.

Franklin D Roosevelt with his military advisers.

leadership style is partly a result of his compulsive avoidance of confrontation. He can't even bring himself to punish his own children, leaving the disciplining to his wife.[11] And partly it is the result of his secrecy, 'The Boss loves secrets', recalled his advisor Sam Rosenmann.

By nature Roosevelt keeps his cards close to his chest. He doesn't have a single true political confidante. There are people he trusts, but they tend to fall out of favour. On a personal level he finds it easier to confide in women than men.[12]

But FDR generates deep loyalty, most conspicuously from his wife, Eleanor, whose affection and esteem for him never leaves her, despite his infidelities and sometimes deprecatory treatment of her and her ideals. There are others like FDR's friend Henry Morgenthau Jr and FDR's female companions Missy LeHand, Lucy Mercer, and Daisy Suckley. The physician who cares for FDR during his last months, Dr Howard Bruenn, remarked later, 'that like all people who work with FDR – I love

[11] W F Kimball, op. cit., p.19.
[12] W F Kimball, interview 16/03/04.

him. If he had told me to jump out of the window, I would do it, without hesitation.'[13]

Roosevelt differs from the other leaders in his war strategy and aims: Stalin, though devious, double-dealing and treacherous in his methods, steadfastly pursues a limited set of aims: to extract the largest possible benefit from the war – territorial, military, diplomatic and economic. Hitler holds a clear-cut yet over-ambitious strategy: German mastery of the European continent. Churchill – patriot and imperialist – firstly desires victory for Britain and then the survival of the British Empire.[14]

Roosevelt is a strange mix of pragmatism and idealism. His policy throughout the war is to use the war as a vehicle to create a working relationship with the great powers that will emerge victorious from this war. And for Roosevelt that is the Soviet Union and United States. He knows that Stalin is a ruthless dictator, but he equally knows that he will need Stalin to help police the world in the post-war order.[15]

Even though Roosevelt and Churchill are close war-time allies, both men are very different in outlook and style. Churchill is an optimist, subjected to bouts of depression, which he calls his 'black dog'. Depression is anathema to Roosevelt, problems deferred are problems solved – for the time being. Churchill is a person of feelings, someone who grapples with a problem by talking about it incessantly. Roosevelt keeps his own counsel, and solves, dismisses or simply ignores problems.[16]

Roosevelt doesn't have a lot of patience for Churchill's diplomatic game playing. For Churchill, an old Victorian imperialist, the intricate details of boundaries and who is in charge of the post-war governments are central questions. Roosevelt on the other hand does not care for details, he is concerned with the general atmosphere in which the post-war order is agreed upon.[17]

In the summer of 1944, the 62 year old Roosevelt dramatically needs a rest, but instead arranges to travel by train and ship from Washington via San Diego to Hawaii for a conference with his two warring Pacific commanders, Admiral Chester Nimitz and General Douglas MacArthur. A trip that requires five weeks, and the result, a two-and-a-half hour conference resolves nothing and ends in a non-decision. The US Navy will continue its western drive toward Japan and the US Army under MacArthur will

[13] D Suckley, diary, 31st March 1945, in WF Kimball, op. cit., p. 18.
[14] J Keegan, op. cit., p.457.
[15] W F Kimball, interview 16/03/04.
[16] W F Kimball, op. cit., p. 22.
[17] W F Kimball interview 16/03/04.

continue with its island-hopping campaign northward from Australia.

FDR has now been ill for some time, his energy levels are down. The turning point in the President's diagnosis comes in March 1944, when a new physician, a cardiologist, is brought to the case: Dr Howard Bruenn.

Until Bruenn, FDR has been feeling up and down, and his

personal physician Admiral McIntire – a nose, ear and throat specialist – was getting nowhere, insisting the President was suffering from influenza and chronic bronchitis. The admiral's procedure of basing his diagnosis on joining the President each morning and watching the verve with which Roosevelt ate his breakfast, is little short of ludicrous. Bruenn diagnoses the President in March 1944 for the first time with advanced cardiovascular disease.[18]

The state of the President's health is strictly being kept secret from the nation. To the press, the Chief Executive suffers from severe bronchitis and seasonal flu.[19] The 'conspiracy' of keeping FDR's illness secret goes as far as to disguise the fact that a well-known and respected Bethesda cardiologist is now attending permanently to the President. Dr Howard Bruenn is carefully

Admiral Chester Nimitz, Commander-in-Chief of the US Pacific Fleet.

[18] R Ferrell, op. cit., p. 27.

[19] Ibid.

cropped out of press pictures, and made to wear a military uniform so he would blend into the President's entourage without raising suspicions, all part of the very conscious effort by the White House publicists to keep FDR's illness a secret.

To some it seems that Roosevelt himself ignores to acknowledge the fact that he is chronically ill. He never asked Dr Bruenn what his diagnosis was in March 1944, nor does he inquire about his blood pressure, which Bruenn measures twice daily, or talks to his family about the state of health. In stark contrast to the hypochondriac Hitler, who watches his own health like a hawk, FDR treats his heart disease with the same disregard as his paralysis.

Nevertheless, Dr Bruenn – who takes over from Admiral McIntire as personal physician to FDR – insists on a strict medical régime. The President is put on life-giving digitalis medication (two pills after each meal), and he is also put on a strict low fat diet. But Roosevelt is very weak during April 1944 – just two months

Reconstruction of FDR with his secretary travelling to San Diego, July 1944.

[20] R Ferrell, op. cit., p. 66.

before D-Day.[20]

A charitable estimate of the time spent each day doing the public business is four hours a day. But it is probably closer to one or two hours. He gets up about noon, sits at his desk, eats a light lunch, works with his secretary Grace Tully, and then goes back to sleep at 6pm.[21] Roosevelt simply can't concentrate for long periods.

*Vice President
Henry A Wallace*

[21] R Ferrell, op. cit., p. 67.

Throughout his life, Roosevelt suffers from blocked sinuses. In regard to the sinus treatments he is looked after by Bethesda practitioner Dr Robert T Canon. Canon treats FDR's nose with Argyrol, a silver packed antibacterial, a simple and effective remedy. Canon would pack the President's nose and place him under a heat lamp, then remove the packs and suction the nostrils clean. Dr Canon visits the President frequently, as often as twice a day. Years later a story circulated that navy physicians used an adrenaline spray, which could have elevated the President's blood pressure. Another story has it that the navy physicians, looking after the President, thoughtfully packed the presidential nose with cocaine.[22]

But by early July 1944, Roosevelt agrees to run for re-nomination. On medical grounds alone, he should not have run. Those who are not in daily contact with him are shocked how thin he has become. He has lost 20 pounds since March.[23] Dr Bruenn is never consulted, but reveals after the war, that if he had been asked then, he would have said it was impossible medically.[24] FDR believes that he has little choice but to run again. Two reasons most probably motivate him: He feels that for the good of the country in wartime he is a better commander-in-chief than anyone else. And secondly, the Democratic Party needs him, for Thomas E Dewey seems a serious – and relatively young – presidential candidate for the Republicans.[25]

FDR's decision to run again, poses an awkward problem to his own party. Several leading Democrats observe how ill he appears without knowing the cause. But it is obvious to them, that whoever is nominated as Vice President will potentially going to be President sooner rather than later. But the party bosses feel they can't talk this over frankly with the President. They would have to say to him 'Mr President, you are terminally ill and whoever is nominated as running mate will have your job before the year is over.' What further complicates the matter is that FDR's traditional running mate Henry A Wallace – an old New Dealer – would be a catastrophe should the President die. Wallace would invariably split the Democratic party.[26]

The dilemma is made worse by Roosevelt's inability to deal with confrontations. He is aware of the problem Wallace poses,

[22] R Ferrell, op. cit., p. 75.

[23] R Ferrell, op. cit., p. 76.

[24] Ibid.

[25] J Bishop, op. cit., p. 97.

[26] J Bishop, op. cit., p. 100.

Churchill, Rooselvelt and Stalin attending the Tehran Conference.

An early photograph of Hitler and Dr Josef Geobbels attending a Nazi rally.

SS guards standing outside Hitler's study in the Reich Chancellery.

Churchill, Roosevelt and Stalin.

After Rooselvelt's death Harry S. Truman continued to attend the conferences with Stalin. At the end of WWII Churchill was replaced by Clement Attlee.

Hitler's with Blondi, his Alsation dog.

Dr Josef Geobbels who, with Major Remer, quelled the officer's revolt in Berlin.

Adolf Hitler in conversation with Reichsführer-SS Heinrich Himmler.

Hitler's personal adjutant Gruppenführer-SS Julius Schaub.

FDR's personal train the 'Ferdinand Magellen'.

Adolf Hitler with Reichsführer-SS Heinrich Himmler.

A reconstruction of Churchill in his bedroom at the War Rooms.

A reconstruction of Hitler, Field Marshal Keitel and General Schoerner at the Wolf's Lair.

The lounge car on the 'Ferdinand Magellan'.

but can't bring himself to deny him the vice presidency. Equally, FDR doesn't want to endorse James F Byrnes, who seems to be too interested in his own advancement. In true Roosevelt style, he tells Wallace that if he was a delegate in Chicago, he – FDR – would vote for him. But then changes his mind and opts for Byrnes. Meanwhile, Bob Hannegan, the Democratic party boss, is weaving the net for an altogether different candidate, Harry S Truman.[27]

Amid all this backroom bargaining, Roosevelt decides to take an extended working holiday on board his personal train. On 4th July, 1944, he sets off from Washington on the 'Ferdinand Magellan' to travel across the States to San Diego, where on the

[27] R Ferrell, op. cit., p. 78.

21st of July he will embark on the USS *Baltimore* to sail to Honolulu. The trip is a chance to try out the role of Commander-in-Chief in the early days of the presidential campaign. There will be a photo-opportunity in Honolulu with Nimitz and MacArthur.[28]

Shortly after 1130hours on Thursday, 20th July, the President's entourage departs from the Oceanside Marine's training exercise. The President drives back to the presidential train parked in a siding in San Diego, feeling unwell.

Meanwhile in Nazi-Germany, Count von Stauffenberg plans to assassinate Adolf Hitler on this day. Could this free the American President to focus all his remaining energies on the ongoing Battle in the Pacific?

[28] J Bishop, op. cit., p. 100-101.

CHAPTER SIX

1200 Hours – Rastenburg

Arming the Bomb

It is not a matter any more of the practical aim, but of showing the world and history that the German resistance at the risk of their own lives has dared the decisive stroke. Everything else is a matter of indifference alongside that.

Major-General Henning von Treschkow 1943

IT is now 1200hours on 20th July, 1944, at Hitler's secret headquarters – the Wolf's Lair – near the Eastern Front. It is a hot and humid day.

In his special barracks, Field Marshal Wilhelm Keitel has called for a pre-meeting in preparation for the Führer's lunchtime situation briefing. Hitler's midday situation conferences are interminably long, and the Führer has been in a foul mood all week. Keitel needs some good news from the Eastern Front, or bad news that he can dress up as good. Keitel is Hitler's closest military advisor – the other officers call him 'Lakeitel' (lackey) behind his back, as he always strives to please rather than tell the truth.[1]

All Keitel's hopes rest on Count von Stauffenberg – who has especially flown in from Berlin. The young colonel will report on raising new troops for the increasingly desperate effort of the German army to halt the Soviet advances. But Stauffenberg, the rising star of the German Army and wounded veteran, has an altogether different agenda, he has come to the Wolf's Lair to kill Adolf Hitler.

Colonel Stauffenberg – Chief of Staff of the Reserve Army – will report on the much needed 'blocking divisions' that the Reserve Army is forming to strengthen the Eastern Front. Unbeknown to Keitel, Stauffenberg is carrying more than the report with him. Alongside with the paperwork, Stauffenberg has four pounds of explosives in his briefcase. Keitel is unaware of the secret mission Stauffenberg is planning: to assassinate his Supreme Commander.

[1] J Fest, interview 13/03/04.

So far, bad luck had dogged all plans to kill the Führer. Hitler   *Field Marshal Wilhelm*
had the luck of the devil.   *Keitel and Adolf Hitler*

A uniform display in December 1943 – during which an
assassination was planned – was cancelled when the train
carrying the uniforms was hit in an air raid and the uniforms
destroyed. Yet another attempt on Hitler's life, on 11th March,
1944, but the assassin, Rittmeister Eberhard von Breitenbuch,
an aide-de-camp to Field Marshal Busche, who intended to

Reichsmarschall Hermann Göring with Adolf Hitler.

shoot Hitler in the head and hid his Browning pistol in a pocket, was on this day not allowed into the meeting with Hitler.[2]

Luck was on Hitler's side and even Stauffenberg began to lose heart. Especially once the Western Allies had established a firm footing on the soil of France. The Gestapo by now also had the scent of the opposition; a number of arrests of leading figures in the opposition pointed to the intensifying danger.[3]

A last opportunity presented itself, when Stauffenberg was promoted to Chief of Staff to the commander of the Reserve Army, General Fromm, in effect his deputy. It provided him with what the opposition, until now, had been lacking: access to Hitler at military briefings. Already he accompanied his superior Fromm to three meetings with Hitler, in order to discuss the raising of new troops through the Reserve Army.

On 6th July 1944 Stauffenberg was called to Hitler's mountain retreat, the Berghof. He carried a large quantity of plastic

[2] J Fest, *Plotting Hitler's Death*, p. 168.
[3] I Kershaw, *Hitler, Nemesis 1936-1945*, p. 670.

explosives undetected into the compound. Fellow-conspirator, Major-General Helmuth Stieff, was then supposed to take it with him into a meeting with Hitler the following day. But Stieff bottled out, and Stauffenberg had to take the explosives back to Berlin, resolved to carry out the assassination himself the following week. This was the crucial turning point, when Stauffenberg decided, that he should be the assassin himself. He no longer wanted to rely on the bravery of others.[4]

On 11th July, Stauffenberg was again summoned to the Berghof, this time to report to the Führer on the formation of a new combat unit to serve on the Eastern Front. He again carried the explosives with him into the meeting with Hitler. But at the last minute he decided not to continue with the assassination attempt, because the leading conspirators had insisted beforehand that Hermann Göring – head of the German Luftwaffe – and Heinrich Himmler – head of the SS – should also be present and must die in the planned explosion.

On 15th July, another briefing was called by Hitler, this time at

Reconstruction of von Stauffenberg and von Haeften arriving at Rastenburg.

[4] E Zeller, *Stauffenberg*, p. 258.

the Wolf's Lair in Rastenburg. Stauffenberg again carried the explosives with him. But when Göring and Himmler again failed to attend, Stauffenberg decided that he would ignite the plastic explosives regardless. However, he had no opportunity to set off the fuse.[5]

It is worth noting that Stauffenberg entered and left Hitler's Head Quarters several times with a briefcase full of explosives without encountering any difficulties. But it is hard to imagine what Colonel Stauffenberg must have felt after these three failed attempts during which he risked his life, and that of his family, and risked being uncovered by Hitler's security staff. By now, he was desperate for his assassination to be successful.[6]

Today on the 20th July, 1944, Stauffenberg can't afford anything to go wrong. This might be the last time that he has the opportunity to assassinate Hitler.

Stauffenberg's decision to carry out the attempt, though courageous is in many ways not the ideal situation. Being severely

Reconstruction of Keitel meeting Stauffenberg

[5] J Fest, op. cit., p. 250.

[6] P Hoffmnann , *Hitler's Personal Security*, p. 246.

disabled after his injuries in the North African Campaign the year before, Stauffenberg is an odd choice. He lost his right hand and two fingers on the left hand. He has lost his left eye, and never got around to get a proper glass eye, but always wore his black eye patch.

Inevitably, Stauffenberg made the choice to be the assassin himself, out of necessity, not because he wanted to, but because there wasn't anybody else in the military opposition who was prepared to do it. His decision to be the assassin increases the opportunity for error.

The other difficulty arising out of Stauffenberg's insistence to be the assassin is that he will be needed at the same time in Berlin to organize the coup. This double role means that the chances of failure are again enhanced. It was far from ideal, but the risk had to be taken. For Stauffenberg all these considerations are immaterial. Today – on the 20th July, 1944, only one fact counts, that Hitler is killed.

His plan is audacious, yet simple. At one o'clock, Stauffenberg will join Hitler during his daily lunchtime situation briefing. He will carry two bombs into the meeting and place the bombs as near as possible to the Führer. On a pre-arranged cue, Stauffenberg will leave the meeting under the pretext to take an urgent telephone call. He will not return, but wait in a safe distance until the bombs go off. Once the bombs have exploded, he will return to Berlin by plane. Meanwhile, the third conspirator, General Erich Fellgiebel, Chief of Signals at the Wolf's Lair, will ascertain that Hitler has been killed by the bombs, and will then call the German Army Headquarters in Berlin to give the signal for the coup to start. By the time Stauffenberg arrives back in Berlin, the coup will be underway and he will join the conspirators in the Army Headquarters in the Bendlerstrasse and lead the coup. At the end of the day they hope to negotiate a truce with the Western Allies, Britain and America.

That, at least, is the plan.

Thursday, 20th July 1944, Stauffenberg arrives at Hitler's compound at around 1100hours, he has to pass two checkpoints to reach the heart of the Wolf's Lair, the inner security perimeter, Sperrkreis I. After a short breakfast in the officers' mess and some telephone calls, Stauffenberg and his personal adjutant Werner von Haeften are greeted by General Walter Buhle and Lieutenant General Henning von Thadden, who are accompanying them to the pre-meeting at Field Marshal

Keitel's barracks, which Stauffenberg believes will finish at 1230hours. That will give him thirty minutes to arm the bombs which he will take into the briefing with Hitler, due to start at 1300hours.

Keitel greets Stauffenberg and tells him that the briefing with Hitler will not take place as usual in the concrete bunker – as the building work still continues – but will today be held in the temporary wooden briefing hut, the so-called Tea-House, an alteration to the schedule, which will have grave consequences for Stauffenberg's plan. Stauffenberg though, being untrained in explosives, doesn't grasp the magnitude of this news and the dramatic implications it will have on his assassination attempt.

During the Keitel pre-meeting, everybody can sense that Keitel is anxious for Stauffenberg to make a good impression in the meeting with the Führer, he virtually rehearses Stauffenberg's presentation with him. Stauffenberg is still unaware of the fact that Hitler has asked for the meeting to be brought forward by half an hour. Stauffenberg's adjutant and co-conspirator von Haeften meanwhile is waiting outside Keitel's office in a hallway. A special missions officer, Staff Sergeant Vogel, will later recall that von Haeften appeared very nervous. He also notices a parcel wrapped in a tarpaulin on the floor. He asks von Haeften what it is, who replies it is for

Hitler being greeted at the Wolf's Lair. The figures of Stauffenberg (far left) and Keitel (far right) are superimposed.

Colonel Stauffenberg's presentation. When Staff Sergeant Vogel returns after a couple of minutes, the parcel and von Haeften have vanished.[7]

Reconstruction of Stauffenberg and von Haeften arming the bomb prior to entering the Briefing room.

Towards noon Hitler's personal valet, Heinz Linge, telephones Keitel's office to remind him that the one o'clock situation briefing has been put forward to 1230hours, because Mussolini is due to arrive at the Wolf's Lair on his special train at 1430hours. Keitel relays the message to the other officers in the meeting.

This is devastating news for Stauffenberg. It means that he has less time to arm the bombs – and there is no end in sight for Keitel finishing off his pre-meeting.

Around 1225hours Keitel is informed that Major-General Heusinger, the General Staff Chief of Operations, has arrived on the local train and is making his way to the Wolf's Lair. Heusinger will start the situation briefing with Hitler with a report on the Eastern Front. His imminent arrival makes Keitel now restless and he tries to hurry the pre-meeting. But at this point Stauffenberg has to try to delay things, to wait, to stay behind if possible. When Stauffenberg planned his assassination attempt, he always

[7] P Hoffmnann, *Stauffenberg*, p. 266-268.

assumed that he would have at least thirty minutes to himself during which he and von Haeften would be able to arm the two bombs. But now Stauffenberg is running out of time, and von Haeften has disappeared. Keitel is urging for the pre-meeting party to make their way to the briefing hut.

In an attempt to delay his departure to the meeting and find the much needed time to arm the bombs, Stauffenberg at this point tells Keitel's adjutant, Major John von Freyend, that he wishes to freshen up after the flight and put a fresh shirt on. This being an extremely hot day, his request doesn't arouse any suspicion, and he is shown to a room in Keitel's barracks where he can change. Stauffenberg also asks the adjutant to call for von Haeften, as he requires help to change his shirt due to his disability.

As soon as von Haeften arrives both men start to arm the bombs. They have brought with them two lumps of 975-gramme German plastic explosives and two British primer charges. Explosive and primer together are so-called adhesive mines, known as 'clams'. The primers come from members of the German Military Intelligence services, who captured them during interrogations of French resistance fighters. The explosives are wrapped in oiled paper and canvas to keep them moist. The bomb explodes when a coiled spring fires a small striker into a detonator. The spring is held in check by a thin wire that is slowly eaten by the acid contained in a capsule. The bomb is primed when the acid capsule is broken by using a pair of pliers.[8]

They are very crude and simple bomb devices, and most crucially they don't have an exact timer. Once the acid capsule is broken and the acid starts eating the wire, the bomb can explode – depending on the outside temperature conditions – anytime between a quarter of an hour to thirty minutes.

For Stauffenberg and von Haeften – this means that time is of the essence.

Stauffenberg and von Haeften are in the room, which was indicated to them by Keitel's adjutant. They immediately start arming the first bomb. Setting the fuses is a cumbersome and tricky task for Stauffenberg. He has a special pair of pliers custom-made for him, to compensate for his disability. One handle has been bent for easier use for a man with only three fingers. Evidently Stauffenberg feels that even though he is disabled, it should be him who sets the fuses rather than the able-bodied von Haeften. Perhaps because he thinks that as the assassin, it is his duty.

[8] P Hoffmann, *Stauffenberg*, p. 264-265; E Zeller, op. cit., p. 259-263.

*Hitler's personal adjutant
Sturmbannführer-SS
Otto Guensche*

To activate the fuse, Stauffenberg has to remove the fuses from the primer charges and squeeze the copper castings to break the glass vials inside, so that the acid seeps into the cotton enveloping the retaining wire. A false angle of pressure, or too much pressure, might break the wire instead of it being slowly corroded to produce the calculated time delay for the bomb. Then he has to determine through an inspection hole that the striker pin is still compressed, remove the safety bolt, and then re-insert the fuse into the primer charges. It is a ticklish job, and even for a man without disability, under time pressure, a tricky feat.

Stauffenberg succeeds in arming one of the bombs.

But then disaster strikes: Staff Sergeant Vogel unwittingly interrupts the two assassins by opening the door. As he tries to open the door, he finds that the movement of the door is stopped by Stauffenberg's body. He sees both men busy with some object, as he gives Stauffenberg the message to hurry up. Stauffenberg answers brusque and agitated, saying that he was on his way. Vogel remains standing in the door-way watching Stauffenberg and von Haeften, then leaves. Vogel doesn't realise then what the two men are up to for a short time but finally Stauffenberg has no way of knowing whether he has been discovered.[9]

Most crucially, there is now no more time to prime the second bomb. Von Haeften hastily puts it into his own briefcase, while putting the one armed bomb into Stauffenberg's briefcase. Their only hope is that this bomb can be placed close enough to Hitler to kill him.

By wanting to take two bombs into the meeting with Hitler, Stauffenberg's intention clearly is to kill everyone in the room. He could not be certain how close the briefcase could be placed to Hitler, so taking two bombs into the meeting would have ensured that everyone present was going to be killed. Now, with only one bomb armed, the positioning of the bomb becomes absolutely crucial.

It is around 1230hours, Hitler has walked from his bunker to the grey conference hut. The day is oppressively hot. As soon as he enters the situation hut, the midday briefing starts. Major General Heusinger begins his report with the situation at the Byelorussian Front. Twenty-four men are in the meeting room, among them two SS men, Hitler's personal aide, Guensche, and Himmler's liason officer with the Führer, Fegelein. The other men are all military men, and two stenographers.

Stauffenberg now has to walk the 300 metres to the meeting hut, as his adjutant von Haeften leaves to arrange for a command car to be on stand-by to drive them both back to Rastenburg airfield once the bomb has gone off.

Outside the barracks, Stauffenberg exchanges angry glances with Keitel's Staff Sergeant, who tries to take the heavy briefcase off the maimed Stauffenberg. But Stauffenberg angrily pulls it back. Later the Staff Sergeant will recall that he admired the energy of the disabled man. But for Stauffenberg it is vital that he places the briefcase in the right spot – to give the bomb a chance to kill Hitler. They both make their way to the briefing hut. Just before they reach the front door of the hut, Stauffenberg suddenly hands Keitel's Staff Sergeant his briefcase and asks him, to place him and his briefcase close to

[9] E Zeller, op. cit., p. 264; P Hoffmann, *Stauffenberg*, p. 265; J Fest, op. cit., p. 255-257.

the Fuehrer, as Stauffenberg's hearing was impaired due to his injuries. He didn't want to miss anything the Fuehrer said, and be up-to-date when it would be his turn to speak to Hitler. Stauffenberg's ploy is for Keitel's Staff Sergeant, who is beyond doubt, to enter the hut with the bomb and place the briefcase. He hopes that his request will ensure the perfect positioning of the bomb.[10]

Reconstruction of Hitler, Keitel and other officers in the meeting room.

It is now about 1235hours.

Stauffenberg has reached the briefing hut and is walking along the hallway to the briefing room. No one asks him to open his briefcase – it is customary for officers to bring their papers and briefcases into meetings with Hitler. Conference participants are also never searched for weapons, although it seems to be customary to leave military caps and pistol belts on a rack outside the room.

The bomb is now on its way. When Stauffenberg enters the briefing room, Major General Heusinger is already presenting the situation on the Eastern Front. Adolf Hitler sits in the

[10] P Hoffmann, *Stauffenberg*, p. 265.

middle of the long map table. All the other officers and generals stand around the table. General Warlimont later recalled the Stauffenberg's entrance:

> *The classic image of the warrior through all of history. I barely knew him, but as he stood there, one eye covered by a black patch, a maimed arm in an empty uniform sleeve, standing tall and straight, looking directly at Hitler who had now also turned, he was a proud figure, the very image of the German General Staff officer – of that time.*[11]

Field Marshal Keitel proudly announces Stauffenberg to Hitler, and explains officiously that he will be reporting later on the new reserve troops. Hitler glances up at him, greets him curtly, but in a rare sign of appreciation, lets Stauffenberg shake his hand. The Fuehrer has heard about the young rising star and war hero. Then he turns back to the maps laid out in front of him on the oak table, and announces brusquely that first he wants to hear Heusinger's report out before being briefed by Stauffenberg.[12]

Meanwhile, Keitel's Staff Sergeant asks the officer standing close to Hitler on his right to make room for the new arrival. Stauffenberg and the briefcase are placed to Hitler's right near the large map table. Now only Heusinger – who stands next to Hitler – separates Stauffenberg from Hitler. Stauffenberg pushes the briefcase with his foot as close to Hitler as he can. The briefcase with the bomb is now only feet away from the Führer. Stauffenberg has succeeded in placing the briefcase as close as possible.

The bomb is in place. The retaining wire inside the bomb has been exposed to the acid for some ten minutes. Stauffenberg knows that he has to find an inconspicuous way out of the meeting. The crucial minutes are ticking away – and he is unsure when his bomb will explode.

After being present at the meeting for a minute or two, Stauffenberg excuses himself, signals to Keitel's Staff Sergeant and mumbles something to him about an urgent telephone call he still has to make before the presentation. Both leave the briefing room, Stauffenberg's departure goes unnoticed, as everybody – especially Hitler – is engrossed in Heusinger's report and the maps. Outside in the hallway, Stauffenberg asks Keitel's Staff Sergeant to call Lieutenant-General Fellgiebel for him. The connection is made, Stauffenberg takes the receiver, and Keitel's adjutant returns back into the meeting room.

[11] Warlimont interview, in P Hoffmann, op. cit., p. 266.
[12] A Speer, *Inside the Third Reich*, p. 525.

Stauffenberg then puts the receiver down, leaves his belt and cap on the rack and leaves the meeting hut.[13]

The acid continues to eat through the retaining wire of the bomb – which is only feet away from Adolf Hitler.

It is 20th July, 1944, 1240 hours.

[13] P Hoffmann, *Stauffenberg*, p. 266-268.

CHAPTER SEVEN

1242 Hours – Rastenburg

A Bomb Explodes

The possibility had never been taken into consideration that a General Staff officer who was summoned to the situation conference would lend his hand to such a crime as an assassination attempt on the Führer.

SS investigation into Hitler's personal security, 26th July, 1944.

Iᴛ is 1240hours on Thursday 20th July, 1944. Adolf Hitler holds his daily midday situation briefing.

The rectangular briefing room in the wooden barrack features, along one side of the room, three windows. In the middle of the room is a long, narrow oak map table, notable for its thick heavy 2inch top and two massive, solid oak table leg supports. On the table are maps from the military frontlines, Hitler's box with coloured pencils, and his old-fashioned steel-rimmed spectacles, which are resting on one of the maps. Hitler is the only one seated; all the other generals and officers are made to stand around the table.

The dictator sits in a wicker-chair in the middle of the long side of the table with the double-winged doors behind him and facing the windows, which are all open to let some much needed air into the room – a very small respite, however, from the sultry midday heat. But it is not only the heat which makes Hitler's generals sweat on this humid summer day. The news from the front is far from good.

The tension in the briefing hut where the situation report was being discussed was nervous, agitated, and at the same time subdued. No-one dared tell Hitler the truth, because the front in the East was wavering and breaking everywhere. And none of his military advisors has the courage to demand a change in strategy from the leader.[1]

Major-General Heusinger has the awkward task of breaking more of the bad news to Hitler. Hitler is toying with a magnifying glass, as Heusinger, standing on his immediate right, reads out the

[1] Interview J Fest, 13/03/04.

glum statistics and points to the relevant parts on the situation map, showing the Supreme Commander where the Red Army has encircled the Wehrmacht and where they have broken through already behind the German defences.[2]

Reconstruction of Stauffenberg in the meeting room, requesting that he stands near to Hitler.

Only a few moments ago, Colonel Stauffenberg left the room to make an urgent telephone call. Now, his absence is noted, as Hitler enquires about the reserve troops. Field Marshal Wilhelm Keitel dispatches his adjutant to find Stauffenberg and bring him immediately back into the meeting room.

Nearly fifteen minutes have elapsed since Stauffenberg armed the bomb. The acid has steadily been eating through the retaining wire holding back the striker pin in the bomb. Any moment the bomb contained in the briefcase, which Stauffenberg has placed close to the Führer under the oak table, can explode.

It is 1241 hours, and Major-General Heusinger continues

[2] W Warlimont, *Inside Hitler's Headquarters*, p. 461.

with his lugubrious report on the latest breakthroughs on the Central Russian Front, when one of the attendees of the meeting, Lieutenant Colonel Heinz Brandt, who stands next to Heusinger, accidentally pushes with his foot against Stauffenberg's briefcase, as he tries to move closer and get a better look at the situation map the meeting is referring to. In order to be able to look at a the map, which is in front of Hitler

Major General Heusinger

and Heusinger, he moves the briefcase further away from Hitler along the table to his own right and places it behind the heavy oak table support.

In a sad irony of the day, this very same Heinz Brandt is actually involved in the military opposition against Hitler, but nobody has told him, that today is the day when Stauffenberg will bring a bomb to the meeting with Hitler. His action of moving the briefcase further away from Hitler will have fatal consequences for himself – and for the plot to kill Hitler.

Heusinger is coming to the end of his report, and has the thankless task of urging Hitler to acknowledge the perilous situation the German Army is in not just along the Central Russian front line, but also on the Northern and Southern front lines as well. The front is breaking, and Hitler's strategy of fighting to the last man is failing abysmally – Heusinger implores Hitler to withdraw the army group.

He is pointing constantly to the situation map spread out in front of him, and the other officers standing around the table have to bend over to study it. At this point during the meeting even Hitler gets up from his seat to find the front lines on the map that Heusinger is referring to. He is now intently leaning far across over the table to check the map. He is propped up on his right elbow, chin in hand, studying the air reconnaissance positions on the map – as the stenographer records what will be the last words of the meeting, delivered by Major-General Heusinger:

Reconstruction of General Fellgiebel in the communications building.

> *The Russians are turning their strengths from Duena northwards. Their advance troops are already south-westerly of Duenaberg. Unless, at long last, the army group is withdrawn from the Peipus-Lake, a catastrophe...*[3]

[3] Stenographers report, in W Warlimont, op. cit., p. 440.

This is the moment when the acid fuse inside the bomb has eaten through the detonating wire and releases the striker pin. Heusinger is unable to finish his sentence. His words are interrupted by a deafening roar and an ear-splitting explosion.

It is 1242hours on Thursday the 20th July, 1944. Stauffenberg's bomb has gone off successfully.

After having excused himself from Hitler's midday briefing only moments ago, Colonel Stauffenberg hurries to meet with his fellow conspirators. He now stands outside building No. 8/13 together with his assistant Werner von Haeften and Signals Chief General Erich Fellgiebel. The three men are waiting for the bomb to go off. As Stauffenberg waits impatiently he must have wondered what is going on inside the meeting room. Has his briefcase been detected? Is Hitler still in the room?

Then suddenly he can hear a massive explosion coming from the direction of the briefing hut. A huge cloud of smoke emanates. The three men can see soldiers and security personnel hurrying

Reconstruction of von Stauffenberg and von Haeften waiting for the bomb to explode.

to the briefing hut. There is chaos and panic in Hitler's compound. Stauffenberg has finally achieved the opposition's aim: a bomb has detonated as planned, and Hitler no doubt has been killed by the blast.

Mission accomplished, Stauffenberg and his aide immediately get into the waiting staff car that has been ordered by von Haeften, ostensibly to take them to lunch with the HQ Commandant, but in reality to take them back to Rastenburg airfield. Time is again of the essence – they have to get out before the security staff close all the gates.[4]

Meanwhile, General Fellgiebel makes his way to the Communications bunker. His task is to ascertain first that Hitler is dead. Once he has confirmation of this, he will telephone the conspirators who are waiting in the German Army Headquarters in Berlin for his call, which will be the crucial signal to issue the 'Operation Valkyrie' orders and telegrams – the start of the army coup. After this vital call, Fellgiebel will disable all incoming and outgoing communications to Hitler's field headquarters.

As Stauffenberg and Haeften ride past Hitler's briefing hut in their car, they can see the huge black cloud of smoke and dust, they see first-aid personnel and other officers running to and fro. Stauffenberg also believes that he sees a person covered with Hitler's cloak being carried from the briefing hut on a stretcher. Later, in five hours time, when he will be back in Berlin, Stauffenberg will testify to his fellow conspirators at German Army Headquarters, that no one present in the meeting room could possibly have survived the bomb blast, and that included Hitler.[5]

But for the moment – Stauffenberg and Haeften have other worries; they still need to get out of the Wolf's Lair, without being stopped or raising suspicion. Under the existing security drill at the Wolf's Lair, all gates have to be shut after an explosion in the compound.[6]

At the inner compound Sperrkreis I check-point, Stauffenberg's disguise works and he can bluff his way through, by pulling rank and saying something about 'Führer's Orders' and highest urgency; the guards should not have allowed him through, as they too have heard the explosion. But they do. The two men pass through.

However, at Wache Süed (southern gatehouse) the outer gate to the compound, Stauffenberg encounters considerable

[4] P Hoffmann, *Hitler's Personal Security*, p. 253.

[5] P Hoffmann, *Stauffenberg*, p. 267. P Hoffmann, *Hitler's Personal Security*, p. 248.

[6] P Hoffmann, *Stauffenberg*, p. 267.

difficulties. The gate is closed, obstacles are blocking the road, and the military guard on duty refuses to let anyone through. All could be lost here, and the two men discovered. But Stauffenberg employs considerable resources of sang-froid and military brusqueness and demands to be allowed to make a call. He is reluctantly granted to enter the guard-house to make a telephone call. He gets through to one of the HQ Commandant's officers, Captain Leonhard von Moellendorf, who he knows and with whom he had breakfast this morning. Von Moellendorf – who is not part of the conspiracy – orders the guard to let Stauffenberg and Haeften pass.[7] Unbelievably, Stauffenberg seems to have succeeded where everyone before him has failed so far: He has killed Hitler and made a clean escape.

Racing in their command car on the narrow road which takes them to the airfield, Haeften throws the second unarmed bomb out of the car into the wood. They proceed to Rastenburg military airfield, where a Heinkel He 111 plane stands waiting for them, engine running. It has been provided by the Quartermaster-General, General Eduard Wagner, who is part of the plot. Stauffenberg and Haeften board and take off at 1315 hours.[8]

The flight to Berlin in a He 111 can take as little as an hour and a half, or as much as two hours with head winds. The commission investigating the assassination attempt on Hitler, later determined the time of landing in Berlin-Rangsdorf as 'towards 1545 hours'.[9]

As the two men fly back it is hard not to imagine the feeling of elation in both of them. Stauffenberg especially must have felt a sense of great relief. He had succeeded in killing the German dictator, the curse of both Europe and Germany.

1242 hours – inside Hitler's situation room.

Suddenly, a massive whitish-yellow flash rockets skyward and a deafening thud shatters the midday quiet. An ear-splitting explosion rocks the room, blowing out the walls and the roof and setting fire to the debris which crashes down on those inside. It is pandemonium. Some of the people in the room are thrown down, hurled or blown across the room. Some have their hair and clothes in flames. Some are pierced and mortally stabbed by the hail of thousands of small and large glass and timber splinters. An

[7] P Hoffmann, *Hitler's Personal Security*, p.249.
[8] P Hoffmann, *Stauffenberg*, p.267.
[9] P Hoffman, ibid..

Hitler showing Mussolini the bomb damage.

inferno of flames is shooting up, plaster rains down on them, clouds of thick smoke billowing up, charred documents spiral down from the sky. The great oak table has collapsed, its top blown to pieces. The room is black with smoke, the floor has buckled up at least 3 feet.

Nicolaus von Below, Hitler's adjutant recalls the moments of the explosion:

> *I was standing a little to the side discussing the agenda for Mussolini's visit with three other adjutants. Heusinger made a point which interested me, and I moved to the opposite side of the table to obtain a better view of the map. I had been there for a few moments when the bomb exploded. I lost consciousness for a few seconds. When I came*

General Günther Korten (left) one of those killed by the bomb blast.

to I saw around me a ruin of wood and glass. My head was buzzing, I had been deafened and was bleeding from the head and neck.[10]

Someone shouts 'Fire!' There are cries for help. Human shapes stumble around the debris, concussed, part-blinded, ear drums shattered, disorientated. In the confusion most of the men try desperately to get out of the ruins of the hut. The less fortunate are buried under the wreckage, some are seriously wounded.

As the dust subsides amidst the devastation, one figure emerges. Field Marshal Keitel rises slowly and stumbles to his feet, waving his arms and shouting. He has survived.

Under the debris a second figure stirs. It is Hitler, lying near the left door-jamb, covered in ceiling lathes, glass-wool insulations and timbers. He can feel his hair and clothes are on fire, his right elbow is hurting savagely. His aides and adjutants

[10] N von Below, *At Hitler's Side*, p. 209.

are fleeing through the doors and windows, as the Führer painfully extricates himself from the wreckage. He weakly stumbles to the corridor, when Keitel notices him, rushes to him, embraces him and shouts:

Mein Führer, mein Führer – you are alive, thank God you are alive.[11]

Both men are covered in dust and wood fibres. Hitler tries to beat out the flames on his trousers. They are in tatters and torn into pieces, which make them look like a hula skirt, beneath

Colonel Nicolaus von Below, Hitler's Luftwaffe adjutant.

[11] A Speer, *Inside the Third Reich*, p. 399.

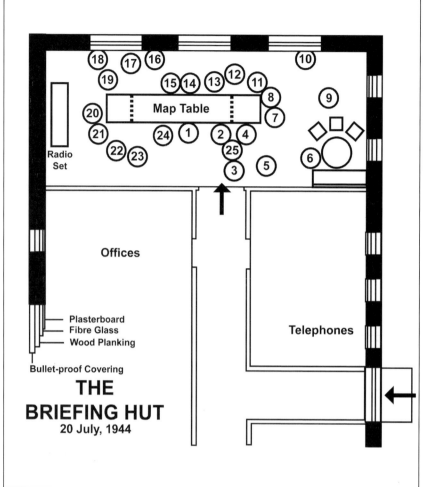

1 - Hitler
2 - Heusinger
3 - Korten {KILLED}
4 - Brandt {KILLED}
5 - Bodenschatz
6 - Waizenegger
7 - Schmundt {KILLED}
8 - Borgmann
9 - Buhle
10 - Puttkamer
11 - Berger {KILLED}
12 - Assmann
13 - John von Freyend
14 - Scherff
15 - Voss
16 - Greushe
17 - Below
18 - Fegelein
19 - Buchholz
20 - Buchs
21 - Sonnleithner
22 - Warlimont
23 - Jodl
24 - Keitel
25 - Stauffenberg

which his long white underwear hangs in shreds. His hair is scorched and tousled, and stands on end like a porcupine's on the back of his head, where the hair is singed.[12]

Supported by Keitel, Hitler makes for the corridor. His right arm hangs stiff and useless, one of his legs has burns, a falling ceiling beam has bruised his back, and his eardrums are burst. Even though he limps, Hitler miraculously is able to walk. One of the other survivors describes both men passing him by as if they were sleep-walking.[13]

The other participants of Hitler's midday briefing have not been so lucky. Twenty-four men had been in the briefing hut when the bomb went off. Eleven of those who had suffered the worst injuries are rushed to the near-by field hospital, just over two miles away. Hitler will visit them the next day and issue a

[12] N von Below, *At Hitler's Side*, p. 381.
[13] Puttkamer in P Hoffmann, op. cit., p. 264.

special military medal to the survivors of the 20th July attempt.

Four men will die: The unfortunate Colonel Heinz Brandt – who moved the briefcase – lost a leg and will die the next day. The stenographer, Dr Heinrich Berger, who sat opposite Hitler and near the briefcase, took the full blast of the bomb. Both his legs are blown off, and he will die later that afternoon. General Günther Korten of the German Air Force, who stood next to Brandt, is stabbed by a spear of wood, and will die the next day. Hitler's adjutant, Major-General Rudolf Schmundt, lost an eye and a leg, and suffered serious facial burns. He will die in the next two weeks. Of those in the briefing-hut, only Keitel and Hitler avoided concussions.[14]

Hitler remarkably survives the bomb blast with no more than superficial injuries. He is taken to his sleeping quarters in his bunker, and his personal physician, Dr Theodor Morell, is summoned urgently to attend to the Führer. Morell later reveals in his diary that he rushed to the Führer's sleeping quarters where he is surprised to find a Hitler who greets him with disdain, saying: 'It's nothing really, it is not as bad as it looks'.

Morell immediately attends to Hitler's injuries. His right forearm is badly swollen and painful, he can barely lift it. There are swellings and abrasions on the left arm, burns and blisters

Valet, Heinz Linge, handing Hitler his service cap and gloves

[14] I Kershaw, op. cit., p. 675.

on both his hands and legs. Hitler's face has been cut in a score of places by the flying splinters, both his eardrums are burst, indicated by the blood seeping steadily from them. The skin on both of his thighs is badly torn by the explosion.

Both of Hitler's legs are littered with wooden splinters from the fragmented oaken trestle. Morell starts to remove the over 100 splinters. Hitler however seems to hardly notice the pain. It seems to Morell that Hitler himself is too baffled about his own lucky escape and survival. Morell recalls that the dictator actually grinned and shouted 'I am immortal! I am invulverable!'[15]

As Morell continuous to dress Hitler's wounds, a panic-stricken Heinz Linge rushes to his master. Hitler's valet has heard that an explosion has shattered the briefing hut. As he approaches the Führer, Hitler greets him with a grim smile on his face and says: 'Linge, someone tried to kill me.'

There is mayhem in Hitler's headquarters, as security officials try to determine who is responsible for the attempt on the Führer's life. Is it foreign agents? Or did one of the construction workers on site use the opportunity of the ongoing building work to try and kill Hitler?

'It was the work of a coward!' Hitler exclaims. His personal adjutant, Colonel Nicolaus von Below – bloodstained and deafened from the explosion, is sent to the telephone exchange. Below removes all the jacks from the telephone switchboard and orders the telephonists not to go anywhere near them.

Shortly after, Hitler learns that the blast wave evidently originated 'above' floor level and within the meeting room. Moreover, only a handful of officers knew that the lunchtime conference had been brought forward because of Mussolini's impending visit to the Wolf's Lair.

Inside his bunker, although badly shaken, Hitler is curiously calm and collected. It seems that he is drawing fresh energy from his miraculous survival. Ironically, the attempt on his life has the unintended consequence of rejuvenating him, and will infuse him with renewed confidence.

On a plane crossing Eastern Europe – the would-be-assassin, Colonel Stauffenberg, is completely unaware that Hitler has survived the attempt on his life.

For Stauffenberg the coup against the Nazi régime has begun.

---

[15] D Irving, *The Secret Diary of Hitler's Doctor*, p. 701

CHAPTER EIGHT

1400 Hours – San Diego
Don't Tell Dr Bruenn

Jimmy, I don't know if I can make it – I have horrible pains.

Roosevelt, 20th July, 1944.

Thursday 20th July, 1944 – after having inspected the 5th Marines amphibious landing exercise – Roosevelt feels the strain of his failing health. The remaining engagements of the day are cancelled. The President is feeling unwell and returns to the *Ferdinand Magellan*, the Presidential Train, which is parked in a siding in the yards at San Diego.

The 'Ferdinand Magellan', FDR's personal train.

The *Ferdinand Magellan* Train was the Air Force One of its time. It was specially designed for Roosevelt by the Pullman railroad company. When the war started, the President's advisors felt that he should have a custom built mode of transport, which offered him maximum protection when he travelled, which he did quite extensively. Roosevelt agreed to the plan under the condition that the train could be used by his successors. His only request for the design was 'to make it a little more comfortable'.

Pullman reinforced the *Ferdinand Magellan* and totally redesigned it: 15mm thick nickel-steel armour plate was riveted on to the sides, floor, roof and ends of the car in a manner that made it undetectable when seen from a distance. The windows were reinforced by 76mm thick bullet resisting glass. At nearly 130 tons weight, the *Ferdinand Magellan* is still the heaviest passenger railcar in the United States.

The number of bedrooms was reduced from five to four, to create more room for a dining-room, a galley kitchen, and the observation lounge. The President entertains his guests in the observation car. The narrow hallways of the railcar are slightly extended – so that the President can manoeuvre his specially designed narrow wheelchair through them with ease. Between the observation lounge at one end and the dining-room at the other, lie the four bedrooms. Lettered A through to D, while room A and D are identical guest rooms, often used by his children, it is bedroom C and D and their interconnecting bathroom which form the Presidential Suite.

Room B is the First Lady's bedroom. It has a single bed, larger than standard Pullman berths, a dresser, closet and wash basin. The connecting bath has a shower, bathtub, toilet, and wash basin. Room C is the President's bedroom. It is the largest and contains, in addition to the standard equipment, a commode chair for the disabled President, and an enlarged bed to accommodate the tall man.

The Presidential Train was the latest in high-tech: ventilation and air conditioning was supplied throughout the compartments. The travelling President has a telephone in each room. When the train is parked in a station, the telephone system is connected to a local telephone company. When the train is moving, it is handled by the Army Signal Corps personnel in the communications car. The mail pouch from the White House is collected whenever the President is stationary and is sent twice daily to the White House.

Even though travelling by train has been made as convenient as

The President's wife
Eleanor Roosevelt

possible for the President, Roosevelt hates the rocking, and has given instruction not to travel more than fifty miles per hour, which increases his travel times. During the night the train always has to be parked in a siding – to allow the President a sound night's sleep.

On Thursday the 13th July, 1944, at 2230 hours, FDR was wheeled aboard his heavy Pullman train by his valet Arthur Pettyman. The train sets off without his wife Eleanor, but with

FDR with his dog 'Fala'.

his whole White House entourage: Admiral William D Leahy, FDR's military Chief-of-Staff, who will accompany him to the meeting with General MacArthur and Admiral Nimitz in Hawaii; Sam Rosenman, the President's speech writer; Vice-Admiral Ross T McIntire – officially his personal physician; Wilson Brown, the President's aide and 'trip historian'; Pa Watson, FDR's appointments secretary; Lt-Commander Howard G Bruenn, the President's real physician and attending cardiologist, disguised as a naval officer; Lt-Commander George A Fox, the President's masseur; Petty Officer Arthur H Prettyman, the President's valet; Grace Tully, the President's secretary; and finally FDR's beloved pet, his Scotch terrier Fala, the presidential dog.

Fala rides in FDR's wheelchair, and travels with the President wherever he goes, on long and short trips, by car, boat or train. He is probably the first celebrity dog. Whenever he is spotted, it is a sure sign that the President isn't far behind. To say FDR is besotted with the dog, is an understatement. FDR and his shaggy black Scottie are inseparable. The President has had pets before, but Fala is his friend in a way no other pet has been. Fala eats with the President and sleeps in a special chair at the foot of Roosevelt's bed. Every morning, Fala has a bone which is brought up on the President's breakfast tray.[1]

Fred D Fair, the President's porter on the *Ferdinand Magellan* train, later recalled waiting hand on foot not only on the President, but also on Fala:

> *I served him his meals, made his beds. We would serve the President 'Highballs' before dinner. Before the meal, I would fix Fala's food. Fala would never go into the dining room until you called him. We'd serve him in there. But you couldn't serve Fala yourself, oh no. You had to hand it to the President, and he'd feed Fala out of his hand. Many times I remember dignitaries and other important folks having to wait for their supper, until Mr Roosevelt finished feeding Fala.[2]*

There were others travelling with FDR in July 1944: three men in a radio pool; nine Secret Service agents, including a strong swimmer, in case anything should happen during the sea voyage; fourteen further protection agents; and eight Navy cooks and waiters are looking after the President's other needs.[3]

The President is undertaking this five week, fourteen-thousand mile military trip to the Pacific Coast, Hawaii and Alaska to inspect troops and confer with his Pacific commanders. This is the official line. In reality, Roosevelt has embarked on this working vacation – consisting of a long slow train trip across the States and a slow voyage on a heavy cruiser – to escape the backroom politics of Washington and the party politics at the Democratic convention in Chicago. Heated debates are raging in July 1944 over who should be his running-mate for the forthcoming presidential elections.

The train journey is an elegant way of avoiding the confrontation brewing. The added advantage is that the train offers an excellent way of arranging to see his mistress, Lucy Mercer Rutherford, en route, without his wife knowing it.[4]

Lucy has been the President's mistress for over 31 years. She joined the Roosevelt staff in 1914 as an assistant to his wife Eleanor. It wasn't before long that the President noticed her charm. But in 1918 Eleanor demanded – her or me – and Roosevelt vowed never to see Lucy again. There are some indications though that the relationship was on and off. But in late June or early July 1944, Roosevelt approached his

---

[1] FDR Library information.

[2] F D Fair, quoted in D K Goodwin, *No Ordinary Time*, p. 324.

[3] As above.

[4] D K Goodwin, *No Ordinary Time*, p. 517.

daughter, Anna, with a whispered request about inviting the recently widowed Lucy to some dinners at the White House. After some deliberations, Anna agreed to make arrangements, she knew that her father was longing for someone to spend the evenings with, someone who listened to him. Lucy's first visit to the White House happened over the weekend of the 7th July,

1944. From then onwards, Roosevelt and Lucy rekindled their affair.[5]

As FDR and the presidential party depart that Thursday evening on the 13th July at 2245hours from Virginia Avenue Station – nobody spots the detour FDR had arranged for. No one remarks that the first train stop will not be Hyde Park – where his wife Eleanor waits for him – but that Mr Roosevelt has pencilled Highland NY, across the Hudson River, as the first stop, near his mistress' stately home Allamuchy, which will allow the President to see her before he goes on the train journey with his wife. FDR knows that Mrs Roosevelt will ask why his train is parked on the other side of the Hudson – and he knows that he will tell her that the Secret Service did not like to have him chance travelling over New York Central's Hell Gate Bridge – which in wartime might be a risk. It will satisfy her. It has before.[6]

After seeing his mistress, FDR spends the Friday of 14th July at his home, entertaining friends and visiting the nearby FDR library, inspecting numerous new exhibits that have arrived since

Allamuchy station where Lucy Mercer Rutherford met FDR's train.

[5] D K Goodwin, ibid.
[6] J Bishop, *FDR's Last Year*, p. 102.

his last visit,[7] only to board the train at Highland again in the evening and embarking on his journey to the West Coast.

The 1944 Democrat Convention in Chicago

FDR succeeds in keeping his renewed secret love affair with Lucy Mercer Rutherford hidden from Eleanor, a secret which will only come to light the day he dies. The train journey however also allows him to keep his options open on the most important political question in July: who should be his vice presidential running mate.

On Saturday the 15th July, 1944, the Presidential train arrives en route to the West Coast in Chicago, where the Democratic Convention will start on the 19th July. The train is moved from Englewood Station to the Fifty-first Street coach yard of the Rock

[7] FDR Day-by-Day; Grace Tully's Appointment Diary.

Harry S Truman who finally won the nomination to run as FDR's Vice President.

Island System, where it is being serviced, train batteries are recharged, and the whole train overhauled for the long trip across the States.[8]

A special telephone connection is set up for FDR to call Robert E Hannegan, the Democratic Party National Chairman, who is already in Chicago to prepare the convention. Shortly after, Hannegan arrives to meet with Roosevelt. The large observation car is cleared for a private conversation. Hannegan is desperate to get a clear signal from Roosevelt who he will

[8] As above.

endorse as his running-mate. FDR's nomination is a foregone conclusion, but the convention is going to see a war over his running-mate. Presidential Advisor James F Byrnes is running, and so is Senator Alben Barkley and Justice William O Douglas, and sitting Vice President Henry A Wallace already claims to have FDR's endorsement.[9] All four men can justifiably say that they at one time or another during the summer of 1944 have been encouraged by the President to run with him.

Until the summer of 1944, Roosevelt managed to keep the disparate elements within the Democratic Party in check. But dissent – which has been kept under wraps – has erupted over the choice of Vice President. Moreover, discontent over Roosevelt has been brewing from the Southern Democrats over his policy to enlarge civil and social rights of 'Negro citizens' and the leftist character of his New Deal. There is also growing objection from several Democrats to the prolonged tenure of one President in office.

Wallace is the overwhelming choice of the 'old' New Dealers, including the President's own wife Eleanor, American labor and many Black activists. But Justice Douglas is the favourite of the right-wing Democrats. Senator Barkley and Byrnes are both the preferred candidates of the big cities, but totally unacceptable to American labor.[10] All four men want to be nominated as Vice

The 1944 Democrat Convention.

[9] J Bishop, op. cit., p. 104.
[10] M Beschloss, *The Conquerors*, p. 112.

Harry S Truman at the 1944 Democrat Convention

Presidents this year – because they all know how ill Roosevelt is, and that they might be President soon.

Party-boss Hannegan on the other hand needs to find a candidate who will bridge the compromise once FDR – the only glue keeping the Democrats together – is gone. Even though Hannegan paints a grim picture of a party divided over the vice presidential question – the President remains ambivalent, insisting that he might support Justice Douglas who played a mean game of poker. FDR doesn't want to admit that there is a problem, and tells Hannegan that he won't lend support to a 'Stop Wallace campaign', equally, he is not going to give his old friend Wallace any help in getting nominated. A typical non-committal Roosevelt move. But Hannegan is determined to get at least some endorsement from FDR. Eventually, the President agrees to sign a letter which in essence says that he would be very glad to run with either Bill Douglas or Harry Truman, since either one would 'bring real strength to the ticket'. The meeting is concluded, and it looks as if nothing has been resolved.[11]

Just before he leaves the train, Hannegan runs back to FDR's secretary Grace Tully, and asks her to retype the letter and to

[11] J Bishop, op. cit., p. 104.

switch the names, so it will read Harry Truman and Bill Douglas.
By naming Truman first, Hannegan hopes it will be plainly
implied that the President favours Truman as his running mate.[12]
It is by this narrow margin that Harry S Truman will become head
of state in April 1945.

FDR's train leaves Chicago shortly after the meeting at
1430hours on 15th July, 1944.

The President instructs his staff that he does not want to reach
his destination San Diego until the pre-dawn hours of July 19th.
It means that the four men who want to run with him have no
chance of getting in touch with him until the opening of the
convention. His instruction also places a huge burden on the
divisional chiefs of the railroads, who have to work out a right-of-
way for the presidential train, with its advance locomotive flying
two white flags, and yet use the tracks allocated to long, slow
freight trains – a logistical nightmare.

On the same day when Hannegan tries to pin the President
down on an endorsement for a Vice Presidential candidate,
Senator Harry S Truman arrives in Chicago for the convention,
accompanied by his wife Bess and his daughter Margaret. Truman
is a firm family man.

Before he left his home in Missouri, Truman received a string
of telephone calls. First off, James F Byrnes told him that he had
FDR's endorsement. Byrnes wanted to make sure that Truman
voted for him. Truman told him that he would be proud to do it.
Then Senator Alben Barkley asked him whether he would
support him. Truman told him that he already pledged to support
Byrnes.

Once in Chicago, Truman starts lobbying for Byrnes. On
Sunday 16th July, he meets Sidney Hillman, the long time
President of the Amalgamated Clothing Workers and a political
force in the liberal wing of the Democrats, over breakfast. To his
surprise Hillman tells him, that he wasn't going to support any of
the four candidates, but instead would vote for him, Truman.

A shocked Truman hurries to the Blackstone Hotel where the
party bosses reside, only to find out that the party line is: 'we have
no candidate'. But personal and party loyalties are important to
Truman, who continues to support Byrnes.

Between Sunday the 16th and Wednesday 19th July the real
convention of 1944 takes place in suite 708/709 at the Blackstone
Hotel, the only room in Chicago with a direct telephone line to the
President – who is travelling. Here the 'Harmony Boys' around
Bob Hannegan are working non-stop to solidify support for their
compromise choice candidate Truman among the party bosses

[12] D Kearns Goodwin, *No Ordinary Time*, p. 527.

Franklin D Roosevelt with Harry Hopkins.

and with FDR. The only person who hasn't been asked yet is Truman himself.[13]

The Presidential Train travels through Kansas City, El Reno, Tucumcari, El Paso, Tucson, Phoenix, Yuma, and finally arrives in San Diego on 19th July at 0200hours in the morning.

Meanwhile in Chicago the backroom politics and political manoeuvring reach a fever pitch as the Convention opens.

Henry Wallace rallies the troops and publicly declares 'I am in this fight to a finish', as Hannegan and his 'Harmony Boys' spread the word that the President favours either Truman or Douglas. Of the two, the party bosses favour Truman, 'the regular guy', against Douglas 'the idealist'.

For Hannegan the political world now hangs on Truman. He decides to ask Truman to run, but Truman declines. Even though Hannegan produces a note, which indicates that the President would be satisfied with either Truman or Douglas. Truman insists that he is pledged to Byrnes, and could not be counted on, unless Byrnes released him. Shortly after this Truman confronts Byrnes with the news from Hannegan's office. Byrnes is distraught and demands to be able to call the President on his train. But the word

[13] R Ferrell, *The Dying President*, p. 78.

James Byrnes

back is: 'The President cannot speak to you at this time.' To Byrnes this clearly is the end of the line and the stab in the back. He withdraws from the race.[14]

But even with Byrnes out of the race, for party boss Hannegan the troubles aren't over yet. The convention roars with 'We want Wallace' shouts. And most crucially, Senator Truman is determined not to run as Vice President.

[14] J Bishop, op. cit., p. 108.

Truman is surprisingly reluctant to accept the party's bid. One reason which later surfaced, when his letters to his wife are published, is that Bess and sister Mary Jane were on his Senate-office payroll, though neither performed clearly defined services.[15]

Hannegan finally devises a ploy to convince Truman that the future of the country and the party depends on him, and that it is the President's wish that he runs for Vice President. Hannegan asks Truman to meet with the other party bosses in suite 708/709 in the afternoon of 19th July. As Truman sits on the bed in the Blackstone Hotel suite, a call comes through from the Presidential Train. The call has been pre-arranged and FDR plays his part.

'Have you got that fellow lined up yet?', Roosevelt asks Hannegan, who replies no. 'Well, tell the Senator that if he wants to break up the Democratic Party by staying out, he can. But he knows as well as I what that might mean at this dangerous time in the world... ' And with these words he slams the phone down.[16]

Truman capitulates, even though he is not clear why his chief prefers him over other, more qualified candidates. But he is finally willing to have his name placed in nomination.[17]

The chronic ambivalence of the President is now as distressing to his party affiliates as to his foreign Allies. If there is something even his closest and dearest friends cannot forgive him – it is his penchant for sudden and irreversible moves. Byrnes and Wallace – the most popular candidates for the ticket – had been actively encouraged by him, both expected to be Vice President, and both felt bitterly disappointed and accused him of hypocrisy.[18]

The dichotomy between the public convention in the Chicago Stadium and the private political convention in the Blackstone Hotel suite 708/709 could not have been more clear. Even as Truman is chosen by the party bosses on this fateful 19th July, Henry Wallace appears on the floor of the convention hall to a roar of adoring approval. The dilemma for the bosses now is how to stop the most probable Wallace stampede the next day, on 20th July.[19]

It is 1400hours on 20th July, 1944. President Roosevelt is still feeling unwell.

[15] R Ferrell, *Choosing Truman*, p. 167.

[16] J Bishop, op. cit. p. 107

[17] R Ferrell, op. cit., p. 168-72.

[18] M Beschloss, op. cit., p. 263.

[19] R Ferrell, op. cit, p. 171.

His son Jimmy – a big, husky Marine himself – is with him. He joined the presidential party the day before, when FDR arrived in San Diego. Jimmy Roosevelt had served in the continuing struggle for Midway. He had been fighting with the support troops at Tarawa and on Guadalcanal following the original landing, when he came down with a severe case of malaria and was sent back to the States. Now, fully recuperated he accompanies his father on the West Coast inspection tour.

Though happy about the reunion with his father, Jimmy can't fail to notice how his father's health has deteriorated.

Franklin D Roosevelt with his dog 'Fala' and one of his grandaughters. This is one of the few photographs showing FDR in a wheelchair.

I saw father alive for the next to last time in July 1944 in San Diego. He was happy to see me recovering from malaria. Although I did not say so, I was sad to see him looking poorly.. He had aged a lot. As commander-in-chief, father had agonized through an awful strain. But I did not think he was dying. That possibility did occur to me, however, when he was stricken.[20]

The two men are talking politics. And FDR tells his son that he is tired. But that he has decided to run again as president, not expecting to have to campaign too hard. He won't be able to take time off from the war to go on the campaign trail. He expects his

[20] J Roosevelt, *My Parents*, p. 276.

running mate to do most of the campaigning. Roosevelt reveals to his son that he doesn't really care who is going to be his vice presidential candidate. 'Truman, Wallace, Byrnes – what does it matter? Let them name someone and get on with it.'[21]

Whether it is the tension of the Democratic Convention in Chicago, the strain of a tiring train trip, a gall-bladder attack, or indeed a minor heart attack or stroke, FDR's pleasant features suddenly tighten to an agonizing frown, and he begins to groan, all colour seems to drain from his face. Jimmy rushes to him, and

FDR with his son, Jimmy Roosevelt.

later recalls his father's collapse in his memoirs:

> *'Jimmy, I don't know if I can make it. I have horrible pains.' It was a struggle for him to speak. I felt more fear than I ever did under fire. I gripped his hand and said I'd call the doctor. He said no, he didn't need a doctor. He lay on his back on the floor of that railroad car for perhaps ten minutes.*[22]

FDR insists that it isn't his heart. He asks Jimmy not to create unnecessary alarm which would jeopardize his chances for re-election.

> *It's easy to say now I should have done what I thought was right, disregarding his wishes, but it was hard then. He was not only my father, he was the commander-in-chief. I did what he wanted done. And minute by minute, as he lay on his back in that train and I knelt alongside him, he seemed to get better. At first his body shook a little. Then it stilled. At first he closed his eyes. Then they opened. The colour seemed to return to his face. He was breathing easier.*[23]

Jimmy's sister Anna later claimed that her brother had acted completely irresponsible, for it would have been his duty to report the incident to Dr Bruenn who was travelling with the President. By collusion or by accident, neither Jimmy Roosevelt nor FDR ever mentioned the attack to Dr Bruenn. The incident only surfaced in Jimmy Roosevelt's memoirs in 1959. During his lifetime, the subject of the President's health continued to be a private matter, which was shared to a certain extent in a light-hearted tone only with his long-time companion, his wife Eleanor, and only the next day.[24]

Dearest Babs

Yesterday Jimmy and I had a grand view of the landing operation at Camp Pendleton, and then I got the collywobbles and stayed in the train, in the p.m. – Better today. Lots of love – back soon.

Devotedly, F[25]

It is a tragic irony that on 20th July, 1944, two of the war leaders come close to death and have a serious medical crisis. If Hitler had been killed by Stauffenberg's bomb the outcome of the war in Europe might have been considerably different; and if FDR's attack had been a more severe stroke, the sitting Vice President, Henry Wallace, would have become President of the United States.

[22] J Roosevelt, op. cit., p. 278.
[23] J Roosevelt, op. cit., p. 279.
[24] J Bishop, op. cit., p. 111-112. R Ferrell, op. cit., p. 79-80.
[25] Letter FDR to Eleanor, 21th July 1944, before departing on USS Baltimore.

While Roosevelt struggles with his ailing health, it is nomination time in Chicago. The Democratic Party is voting for their next presidential candidate. Would the delegates have voted differently, had they known how ill their Chief Executive really was?

Party-Boss Robert Hannegan, meanwhile, has other worries. The election of FDR is a formality. Hannegan has to make sure that Truman is elected as Vice President.

But sitting Vice President Henry Wallace has other plans.

His supporters have invaded the Chicago Stadium – many with fake tickets – and are packing the galleries. They intend to stage a massive pro-Wallace demonstration and get their hero nominated and elected on the same night as FDR.

CHAPTER NINE

1500 Hours – Rastenburg

Providence

Duce! I just had the most enormous stroke of good fortune!

Hitler to Mussolini, 20th July, 1944.

THURSDAY, 20th July, 1944 – at about 1315hours – merely half
an hour after the assassination attempt – Hitler re-emerges
from his bunker into the midday sunshine, wearing a fresh
uniform over bandages that cover all injuries, except for those to
his head. Hitler's valet, Heinz Linge, helped him to undress.
Linge later recalled that this was the first and only time during his
years in Hitler's service, that the Führer allowed Linge to see him
naked.[1]

The news of the explosion spreads to the secretaries. Traudl
Junge later recalls the events:

> *We had heard the explosion, but we thought it was a wild animal
> which might have triggered one of the many land mines in the outer
> security area. But then an officer told us the news 'A bomb has gone off
> next to the Führer!' We stood there like two lambs during a heavy storm,
> not knowing what to do. Suddenly, Christa asked: 'What will happen to
> us if Hitler is dead? And who will take over?' We both jumped up and
> tried to get to the situation barrack to gain more information. ... Then
> we went to the Führer's bunker. And there he was, I nearly had to laugh,
> because his hair that usually was so well kept, was standing on end. But
> he greeted us smiling and said:*
>
> *'Well my ladies, this went well yet again, another proof that
> providence has chosen me to see through my mission. Otherwise I would
> be dead by now.'[2]*

There are ample reasons for cancelling the scheduled visit of
the Italian Fascist leader Benito Mussolini: Hitler's medical and
mental condition, and, most of all, the necessity to review and
perhaps change the security procedures at the Wolf's Lair.

[1] H Linge, *Bis zum Untergang*, p. 226.
[2] T Junge, *Bis zur letzten Stunde*, p. 145-146.

Hitler's trousers are
displayed for the benefit
of the press.

Nothing of the sort is done, the day goes ahead as planned. Security officers however seal off the briefing hut where the bomb had gone off. Hitler's bunker is carefully searched for more devices, and alert conditions are given out to all the security gates.[3]

But Hitler's instructions are to go ahead with the day as scheduled, as his secretary, Christa Schroeder, vividly remembers these hours and Hitler's exhilaration:

[3] P Hofmann, *Hitler's Personal Security*, p. 252.

I did not expect to be called in for lunch with him after the assassination attempt. But nonetheless I was sent for by the boss to join him. I was astounded to see how fresh he looked, and how sprightly he stepped towards me. ... 'If this explosion had happened in the bunker nobody would have survived. But didn't I tell you before, that I had suspicions that something like this might happen? Didn't I tell you only yesterday, do you recall?'[4]

He asked her whether she had seen the destroyed meeting room yet. When Christa Schroeder replied that it was still cordoned off, Hitler asked his valet to bring the uniform, so she could at least have a look at this.

Hitler meets Mussolini at the Rastenburg station on July 20, 1944. Hitler greets him by shaking with his left hand as his right has been injured in the bomb blast.

He showed me the trousers which were almost in total shreds. He seemed to be strangely proud of this trophy. And then he asked me to send it as a memento to Eva Braun at the Berghof with the instruction to look well after it.[5]

[4] C Schroeder, *Er war mein Chef*, p. 147.

[5] Ibid.

His miraculous survival seems to have confirmed to Hitler that he was chosen after all by destiny to lead Germany to victory, as Christa Schroeder recalls:

> *He told me how his servants had reacted to the news. Heinz Linge was indignant and others had cried. Then he said verbatim: 'Believe me, this is the turning point for Germany. From now on things will look up again.' I told him he couldn't possibly go ahead with the meeting with the Duce. 'On the contrary!' he retorted, 'I must — what would the world press say if I did not!'*[6]

The Duce's visit is scheduled for 1430hours. But the Italian leader is late. Their meeting on this fateful 20th July, 1944, will be their seventeenth — and last. It certainly is their strangest meeting.

Hitler drives to the nearby train station, built especially to accommodate the arrival of the Führer's own train, but also the trains of high dignitaries. After the sultry heat of the morning — a short yet heavy summer-thunderstorm pours down on Adolf Hitler, just as he stands on the platform waiting for Mussolini's train to pull in. The Führer wears a black cape over his uniform, and his right arm is in a sling. He greets Mussolini with his left hand.[7]

Mussolini's train is delayed because of the increased security checks following the bomb blast. Hitler's German translator, Paul Schmidt, later recalled the difficulties he had himself in reaching the meeting.

> *'Even if the Emperor of China had issued you a pass, I would not let you through' said the guard, at the outer security perimeter, to me. 'But you know me', I said, 'I am the translator and have to be there when the Duce arrives at 3pm.' I asked him why he couldn't let me pass, and he simply snarled at me 'Because of the incident'. That's when I knew that something out of the extraordinary must have happened.*[8]

Eventually, translator Schmidt is allowed through, only to record the bizarre conversation taking place between Hitler and the Duce:

> *Hitler spoke with a strangely calm and monotonous voice. 'Duce! I have just had the most enormous stroke of good fortune', Hitler said in greeting his Italian guest. He told a shocked Mussolini what had happened.*[9]

[6] C Schroeder, op. cit., p. 148.

[7] U Neumaerker, R Conrad, C Woywodt, *Wolfsschanze*, p. 14; see also the German newsreel film showing the event.

[8] P Schmidt, *Statist auf diplomatischer Bühne*, p. 135.

[9] Ibid.

The entourage then make their way to the Wolf's Lair where Hitler shows Mussolini the destroyed situation hut. Accompanied by the interpreter, Hitler describes to the Duce exactly where he stood, right arm leaning on the table, as he studied the map, when the bomb went off. Hitler shows him the singed hair at the back of his head. In a macabre scene, the two dictators sit down on upturned boxes amidst the debris of the destroyed hut. For a few moments neither dictator said a word.

Then Hitler said in a quiet voice:

> *When I go through it all again ... I conclude from my wondrous salvation, while others present in the room received serious injuries ... that nothing is going to happen to me.*[10]

Nursing his injured right arm Hitler in the company of Mussolini (far left), Martin Bormann, Admiral Dönitz, Hermann Göring and Hermann Fegelein, Hitlers SS adjutant and brother-in-law. Fegelein married Gretl Braun, sister of Eva, in June 1944.

Hitler sees his survival as the potent sign from providence that he and Mussolini will be able to bring their common cause to a victorious end.[11]

For a while the Duce and his entourage are left to their own devices, as Hitler receives first reports on who might be behind the bomb. Martin Bormann, Hitler's indispensable enforcer, relays the report of Sergeant Arthur Adam who tended the telephone outside the situation briefing room, and saw the one-armed Colonel Stauffenberg leave the lunchtime briefing in a

---

[10] Ibid.
[11] See I Kershaw, *Hitler, Nemesis 1936-1945*, p. 684.

hurry just before the explosion, without his briefcase, cap and belt. Sergeant Adam's report is at first rejected by other army officers because of the implied libel against the worthy Stauffenberg. But Sergeant Adam approaches Bormann, who takes him to see Hitler personally.

One piece of evidence is found within the debris. Gestapo investigators find shreds of Stauffenberg's yellow leather briefcase embedded in the wreckage. And so one piece of evidence quickly leads to the next, by mid-afternoon leaving no doubt among the Führer's staff who planted the bomb. They don't realize however the enormity of the conspiracy or that a coup d'état against him and the régime is under way in Berlin.[12]

Somewhere in the skies between Rastenburg and Berlin two planes are flying in opposite directions.

On the one plane the head of Reichs Security Headquarters (RSHA), *Oberstgruppenführer-SS* Ernst Kaltenbrunner, and the superintendent of the police, Bernd Wehner, are flying from Berlin to Rastenburg to take over the political and technical investigation of the assassination attempt. On the other plane, a Heinkel He 111, the assassin Colonel von Stauffenberg and his adjutant Werner von Haeften are flying from Hitler's Headquarters back to Berlin to start the army coup against the Nazi régime.[13]

After having planted the bomb, Stauffenberg now finds himself condemned to more than two hours of anxious waiting as he travels back to army headquarters in Berlin. His only hope is that the other conspirators – who hold the levers of power now – will be successful in implementing their coup plans, codenamed 'Operation Valkyrie'.

But the success of the coup hinges on the third conspirator at the Wolf's Lair, signals chief, General Erich Fellgiebel. His duty is to call the conspirators in Berlin and give the signal for the coup to start, once Hitler's death is certain.

General Fellgiebel is waiting in front of the Führer Bunker to ascertain whether Hitler is dead or alive. It is about 1315hours. He knows the bomb has gone off, but he doesn't know how serious Hitler's injuries are. It must have been devastating for Fellgiebel, when he sees Hitler emerging from the bunker – dressed in fresh clothes and hardly injured. What went wrong? And what is he to do? Do the Führer and his security personnel already know who was behind the bomb? Some witnesses report that Fellgiebel

[12] P Hofmann, op. cit., p. 253.
[13] J Fest, *Plotting Hitler's Death*, p. 262.
[14] P Hoffmann, op. cit., p. 252.

Reconstruction of General Fellgiebel telephoning Berlin to tell the other plotters that Hitler was dead.

immediately congratulates Hitler on his survival.[14] In this moment, Fellgiebel could have finished Stauffenberg's work by shooting the Führer, there and then.

Now that it is clear to Fellgiebel that Hitler has survived he needs to act swiftly to contact the conspirators at army headquarters in Berlin with the news and then disable communications. But, unbeknown to him, Hitler's adjutant Nicolaus von Below has already rushed to the communications bunker to enforce a news black-out immediately after the bomb blast:

> *I ran to the signals barracks and passed orders to the duty officer to block all outgoing signals except those from Hitler, Keitel and Jodl. Then I went to the Führerbunker where I found Hitler sitting in his room. As I entered I saw that he had the facial expression of a person who has faced death and come through it almost unscathed.*[15]

Fellgiebel now walks over to the telephone-exchange bunker, only to find that his own assignment coincides with the interests of the surviving Hitler régime. As Signals Chief, he confirms the news blackout, which remains in place for more or less the next two to three hours. Which means that all regular telephone and teletype connections are blocked, cutting off anybody within the

[15] N von Below, *At Hitler's side*, p. 209-210.

Obergruppenführer-SS
Ernst Kaltenbrunner.

Wolf's Lair from communicating with the outside world, without prior approval by the highest authorities.

The second part of Fellgiebel's assignment, informing the other conspirators in Berlin, is trickier. He is one of the few high ranking officers who still has unhindered access to the telephone, but the crucial question is: what shall he tell his fellow conspirators waiting in Berlin?[16]

General Fellgiebel has two options open to him. He can hide the fact that Hitler is alive, do everything possible to maintain news

[16] P Hoffmann, *Stauffenberg*, p. 268.

blackout for incoming messages, resorting to violence if necessary, and give the conspirators a fighting chance to kick-start the army coup from Berlin during these vital hours of confusion in the Nazi Reich. There is a good chance that with Hitler and the other leaders being cut off in the Wolf's Lair the army officers' coup in Berlin can still succeed. The second option open to Fellgiebel, is to tell Berlin that Hitler has survived and to immediately abort the coup altogether. After all, he knows that maintaining news blackout will be difficult.[17]

In the end, Fellgiebel opts for a third way. At around 1325hours he calls Major-General Fritz Thiele, communications chief at army headquarters in Berlin. It is a bad line, and Fellgiebel leaves the following cryptic message:

> *Something terrible has happened. The Führer is alive.*[18]

Then he puts the phone down and maintains the news blackout. Fellgiebel later testified that he believes that he has told the fellow conspirator in Berlin that the assassination has failed, but has also given them to understand that the coup should proceed nonetheless.[19]

But as it turns out, Fellgiebel's message leaves the conspirators in Berlin more confused then clear. What did his message mean? Did it mean the bomb had gone off? Or did it mean the bomb hadn't gone off? Had Stauffenberg been prevented from placing the bomb, as happened a few days earlier? Or had Stauffenberg been found out? Had they been found out too? Had Stauffenberg been arrested? Was he still alive? Should they continue with the coup regardless? Should 'Operation Valkyrie' go ahead?[20]

Fellgiebel's message so throws fellow conspirator Thiele – that he decides to go for a walk – to clear his mind – without bothering to inform the other conspirators about this vital telephone message from Hitler's Headquarters.[21]

At around 1400hours another message from another of Hitler's frontline headquarters, 'Mauerwald', reaches fellow conspirator Major General Friedrich Olbricht: there has been an assassination attempt on Hitler, but it failed. More confusion. But more importantly it exposes a crucial flaw in their plan, they never considered Plan B: the bomb explodes, and Hitler survives.

Finally Thiele returns from 'his walk' at around 1515hours. The news blackout at the Wolf's Lair has just been lifted by SS-Chief Heinrich Himmler. All communication lines are now under direct

[17] J Fest, op. cit., p. 261.
[18] P Hoffmann, *Stauffenberg*, p. 268.
[19] J Fest, op. cit., p. 261.
[20] I Kershaw, op. cit., p. 675.
[21] J Fest, op. cit., p. 263.

Fellgiebel in the Communications Room. (Reconstruction)

control of the SS.

Thiele calls the Wolf's Lair and tries to gauge more information. He is told that an explosion in the conference room at Hitler's headquarters has left a large number of officers severely wounded. Thiele believes that his source also implies, between the lines, that the Führer is seriously injured or even dead.[22]

The conspirators in Berlin now confer for the first time. Assessing Fellgiebel's earlier confusing message, taking into consideration that the assassin and leader Stauffenberg is still airborne, and that the news blackout is partially lifted, the conspirators desperately try to figure out what they should do. As the vital minutes and hours tick by, the two key conspirators Major General Olbricht and Albrecht Mertz von Quirnheim now decide to issue the 'Operation Valkyrie' orders, on their own if necessary.

Meanwhile, the two men who planted the bomb and were there when it exploded, Colonel Stauffenberg and his adjutant Werner von Haeften, arrive at Rangsdorf Military Airfield near Berlin around 1545hours. But because of a mis-communication – they were expected to arrive at Tempelhof airfield – there is no command car waiting for him. However, around 1600hours

General Friedrich Olbricht (left) and Mertz von Quirnheim.

Haeften calls the fellow plotters from the airfield and reports that the bomb has been successful and Hitler is dead.[23]

It is now almost four hours since the assassination attempt – and the conspirators are none the wiser what to do. Some of them argue to wait for Stauffenberg to report to them in person, others advocate to issue the 'Valkyrie' orders anyway – as too much time has been wasted already.

Growing ever more impatient with their weak-willed fellow officers, Major General Olbricht and Mertz von Quirnheim approach the Head of the Reserve Army, General Friedrich Fromm, and ask him to approve the orders for the first stage of their rebellion to be sent out. But Fromm tells them that he will only approve these orders if he has confirmation of Hitler's death.

At around 1610hours Fromm takes the initiative and picks up the phone. To his surprise he is immediately put through to Hitler's Chief of Staff, Field Marshal Keitel, who is meeting with Mussolini's Marshal Graziani. Keitel confirms to Fromm that an attempt on the Führer took place, but also tells him the devastating news that Hitler is alive and at the moment conferring with Mussolini. Keitel also asks Fromm 'By the way, where is your

[23] P Hoffmann, *Staufenberg*, p. 267.

Chief of Staff, Colonel Stauffenberg?'
Fromm tells Keitel, that Stauffenberg still hasn't arrived.[24]

Field Marshal Erwin von Witzleben (left) and General Erich Hoepner.

Unsurprisingly, Fromm – who up until now had watched the activities of the army conspirators from the sidelines – absolutely refuses to countersign the 'Valkyrie' orders, and distances himself from the conspirators.

Colonel Stauffenberg and Werner von Haeften finally arrive at the army headquarters in Berlin at around 1630hours. They both expect to find a major army rebellion to be in full swing, instead he finds his fellow plotters in turmoil. When he enters his office in the Bendlerstrasse, he finds many of the officers distancing themselves from the coup and dithering, and a few officers pushing ahead with issuing 'Operation Valkyrie' orders to the regional army commanders which started with the sentence 'The Führer Adolf Hitler is dead.' They had issued them without General Fromm's approval.

The atmosphere in the Bendlerstrasse is at fever-pitch as Stauffenberg makes his way to his superior, General Fromm, to convince him to join the coup. Stauffenberg insists that Hitler is dead. He had witnessed the explosion himself and seen Hitler being carried out on a stretcher. When Fromm questions him

[24] P Hoffmann, *Staufenberg*, p. 267.

further as to how he can be so sure, Stauffenberg exclaims 'Because I planted the bomb. Nobody can have survived the blast.' Fromm is flabbergasted – or, at least, seems to be. With mounting rage he relays his own telephone conversation with Keitel just a few minutes ago, to which Stauffenberg replies exasperated: 'Keitel always lies through his teeth.'

Unimpressed by this, Fromm makes up his mind and declares Stauffenberg and the other conspirators under arrest. Pistols are drawn and in the ensuing fight Stauffenberg overwhelms Fromm, puts him under arrest in his office, and assumes the leadership in the coup.[25]

Stauffenberg insists that more copies of the orders should be transmitted by tele-printer. But the Valkyrie orders are long and have to be typed on the Enigma encoding machines. This takes hours, only four secretaries are cleared to send secret tele-printer messages, and it takes them a further three hours to transmit the text. Without the secrecy requirements the messages could have been sent at greater speed through more than 20 tele-printer machines. Yet again the plot of the renegade German officers seems to fail because they did not attend to the minor details and practicalities of how to overthrow the regime.[26]

In all the confusion of reports, whether Hitler is dead or not, the younger officers clearly decide to go ahead with their planned rebellion. It doesn't seem to matter any longer, whether Hitler is alive or not. The ill-fated coup is on autopilot.

At 1700hours tea is served in the headquarter's mess at the Wolf's Lair. Hitler subjects Mussolini to the usual barrage of impressive statistics of his war minister, Albert Speer, on the forthcoming production of new tanks, guns, and ammunition. Hitler also secretly confides that soon there will be a new weapon, the V-2 rockets. He is resolved to 'raze London to the ground' – and 'after August, September, or October' the new secret U-boats will also enter service.[27]

As the two dictators sip herbal tea and munch biscuits – most extraordinary tele-messages are decoded by the signals officers in the communications bunker.

The orders seem to emanate from the office of the Head of the Reserve Army, General Fromm, and are directed at the territorial army commands (*Wehrkreise*). The orders proclaim a state of emergency under the codename 'Operation Valkyrie'. By

---

[25] E Zeller, op. cit., p. 272.
[26] J Fest, op. cit., p. 266.
[27] I Kershaw, op. cit., p. 677.

Reichsminister Josef Goebbels.

telephone too the commands are being instructed that Field Marshal Erwin von Witzleben is now Supreme Commander of the Wehrmacht and that he has appointed General Erich Hoepner as commander of the home forces.[28] The emergence from obscurity of these forgotten and forcibly retired, or cashiered army officers can only mean that an army putsch is being attempted in Berlin.

Tragically, the renegade Generals did not realise that a special network feeds all orders issued to the territorial army commands automatically to the Führer's headquarters as well. This slip is crucial to the crushing of the putsch.

[28] J Fest, op. cit.p. 267.

Actors playing Keitel and Hitler before digitally enhanced.

Actors playing Churchill and Ismay before digitally enhanced.

A set scene of the 'Ferdinand Magellen'.

The actor playing FDR after digital enhancement.

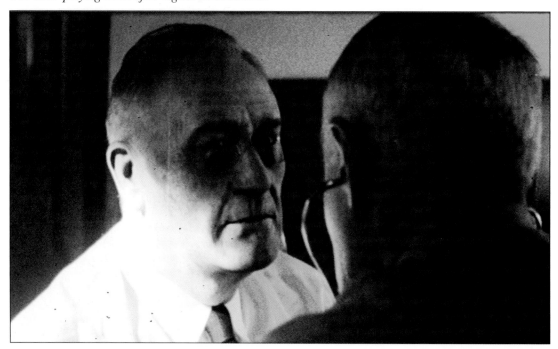

Churchill before enhancement ...

... and after.

The actor playing Hitler after enhancement.

The actor playing FDR before digital enhancement.
The three actors playing FDR (middle), his doctor and son.

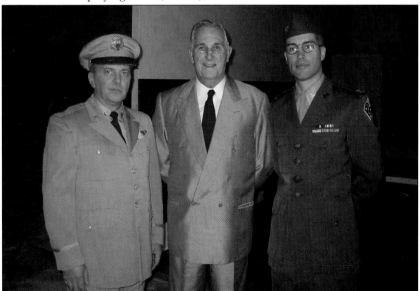

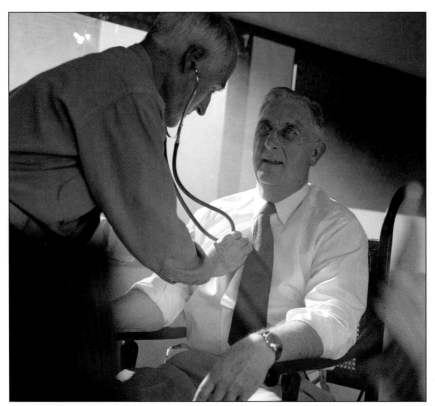

All the actors were chosen for their physical similarities to the various people portrayed in the drama-documentary, but facial attributes were added later.

The actor playing Stalin ...
... and FDR.

Hitler at the map table (reconstruction).
Actors and film crew on one of the sets.

The counter measures from the Wolf's Lair, on the other hand, are fast and decisive. Since General Fromm, on the face of it, seems to be part of the army conspiracy. Hitler decrees that SS-Chief Heinrich Himmler now controls all army units of the Reich. The Gestapo is empowered to arrest the rebel officers. Hitler orders a succinct communiqué to be broadcast immediately to the German People and drafts it along the lines of:

> *A bomb attack was made on the Führer today. ... Apart from minor burns and bruises the Führer is uninjured. He resumed work immediately afterward and as planned received the Duce for lengthy discussions.*

Hitler relays it to his Propaganda Minister Joseph Goebbels in Berlin for immediate circulation to the national German radio station.

Field Marshal Keitel, furthermore now issues a dramatic message, which will crush the rebellion even before it begins. His message to all the territorial army commands reads:

> *Most Immediate! The Führer is alive! Safe and sound! Reichsführer SS new commander of the Reserve Army, only his orders valid. Do not obey orders issued by General Fromm, Field Marshal von Witzleben or General (ret) Hoepner. Maintain contact with the local party Gauleiter and police commander!*

However, more messages from the renegade Generals arrive at the Wolf's Lair. This time they are authorised and signed by Colonel von Stauffenberg, who in effect has now signed his own death-warrant.

Hitler's secretary, Christa Schroeder, recalled the events of the afternoon tea and Hitler's first outburst:

> *When we met up with Hitler for the traditional afternoon tea, the first news came in about Stauffenberg. Hitler was very angry that Stauffenberg had been able to escape to Berlin. But when he was told that this way all the other conspirators were in one place and could be arrested, he was very satisfied.*
>
> *'Now I am calm. This is the salvation for Germany. Now I have the swine hunds who for years have sabotaged me. Now I have the proof that the whole German High Command was poisoned. These criminals they wanted to kill me, they don't know what horrific things would have happened to Germany if they had succeeded. They don't know the plans of our enemies, who want to destroy Germany so much that it will never rise again. This war needs to be won by us, otherwise Europe will be lost to Bolshevism. And I will make sure that nobody stands in my way. I am the only one who truly understands the danger we are in and the only*

[29] C Schroeder, *Er war mein Chef*, p. 148-149.

one who can turn the tide around.'[29]

Further alarming news reaches Hitler at the Wolf's Lair from the Reichs Chancellery in Berlin. Strange events are afoot. Streetcars are rattling through the government quarter without stopping and the area is being cordoned off by the troops of the city battalion. Fearing that he is losing control of events in Berlin, Hitler phones Joseph Goebbels to find out what has happened to his press communiqué. Goebbels replies that he is sitting on it until he has composed a fitting commentary to go with it.[30]

At this point Hitler explodes in anger:

> *I didn't ask you for a commentary. I just want the news broadcast as fast as possible.*

At 1828 hours the German radio service is interrupted with the startling news flash. It deals the fatal body-blow to the coup. This is also the first official news to reach the German people.

---

[30] J Goebbels, *Diaries*, Vol 23, p. 684.

CHAPTER TEN

1700 Hours – London

Your Enemy's Enemy

…the Gestapo and the SS have done us an appreciable service in removing a selection of those who would undoubtedly have posed as 'good' Germans after the war. …It is to our advantage that the purge should continue, since the killing of Germans by Germans will save us from future embarrassments of many kinds.

John Wheeler-Bennett memorandum to Churchill 25th, July, 1944

Thursday, 20th July, 1944 – it is 1700hours and Prime Minister Winston Churchill is keeping to his daily routine by having his afternoon nap. He is unaware of the failed assassination attempt on his enemy's life. But that something is under way in Nazi Germany seems to become more and more apparent when around 1700hours BBC Monitoring picks up the first radio communications about internal upheavals in Berlin. Throughout the afternoon reports arrive from neutral Sweden that telephone and telegraph communications to Nazi Germany's capital Berlin are suspended.[1] Nobody is for certain however what has occurred.

Remarkably, Churchill's war-time enemy Hitler survives this attempt. Even more remarkable is that Hitler survived at least forty-six attempts on his life between 1921 and 1945. There was no shortage of would-be assassins from the opposition within Nazi Germany.[2] But when a bomb explodes on the 20th July, 1944, the first suspicion among Hitler's entourage is that a British agent threw a bomb through the open windows of the meeting hut.

So how advanced were British Secret Service plans in July 1944? Did Churchill authorise assassination attempts on Hitler? Did he support the German assassination attempt on the Führer? Or are Hitler's enemies also Churchill's?

Ironically, Hitler's initial suspicions in July 1944 are not too far away from the truth. Special Operations Executive (SOE),

[1] R Lamb, *Churchill*, p. 291.
[2] P Hoffmann, *Hitler's Personal Security*, p. 268.

Britain's secret organisation aiding resistance movements during the Second World War, does indeed plot to assassinate him. A small department within SOE, Section X, formed in November 1940, has the task of investigating, how, when and where an assassination could be done. Only the staff of Section X and a few principal SOE officers know about this Top Secret project, which is codenamed 'Operation Foxley'.[3]

General Sir Hastings Ismay (left) and General Colin Gubbins.

Probably in June 1944, Section X is encouraged by highest political and military leaders to intensify the planning of 'Operation Foxley'. All available information on the German dictator's travel arrangements, lifestyle, and daily routine are meticulously collated.

The reason for this heightened activity is a report from an Algiers agent, received on 20th June, 1944, in SOE's London Headquarters in Baker Street. The report argues for an immediate killing of Hitler. The source of this astonishing report is a French colonel who claims that Hitler is hiding in a castle near Perpignan until 24th June. Even though the facts are most improbable, SOE acts swiftly, and SOE Chief General, Colin Gubbins, sends a letter marked 'Top Secret' to Churchill's Chief of Staff, General Sir Hastings Ismay, in which he asks

[3] D Rigden, *Kill the Führer*, p.1-2.

First page of the 'Operation Foxley' memorandum.

Operation.
FOXLEY.

INTRODUCTION.

1. **Object:** The elimination of HITLER and any high-ranking Nazis or members of the Führer's entourage who may be present at the attempt.

2. **Means:** Sniper's rifle, PIAT gun (with graze fuze) or Bazooka, H.E. and splinter grenades; derailment and destruction of the Führerzug by explosives; clandestine means.

3. **Scene of operations:** The most recent information available on Hitler and his movements narrows down the field of endeavour to two loci of action, viz. the BERCHTESGADEN area and the Führerzug (Hitler's train).

The BERCHTESGADEN area includes the OBER-SALZBERG as well as the road from the BERGHOF (Hitler's residence on the OBERSALZBERG) to SCHLOSS KLESSHEIM, one of the alternative Führerhauptquartiers which were set up in Germany following the threat to the RASTENBURG (East Prussia) FHQ by the advance of the Russian armies in Poland.

Loci of action in connection with the Führerzug include the SCHLOSS KLESSHEIM sidings, SALZBURG railway station and the routes followed by Hitler's train when travelling north (to Berlin) and west (to Mannheim).

'whether the Chiefs of Staff would approve the immediate execution of Hitler should it prove to be practicable'. Gubbins concludes:

It may be argued that to kill Hitler would turn him in the eyes of the Germans into a martyr. On the other hand, I feel that his removal would certainly shorten the war considerably. I am naturally giving instructions for the project to be investigated in the greatest detail but if meanwhile you could obtain for us a decision on the question of principle whether we should be allowed to carry out this project or not, I should be most grateful.

Ismay replies on 22nd June with a top secret and personal letter and a telephone conversation. The letter encloses a minute which Ismay sent to Churchill the day before. The minute said:

The Chiefs of Staff were unanimous that, from the strictly military point of view, it was almost an advantage that Hitler should remain in control of German strategy, having regard to the blunders that he has made, but that on the wider point of view, the sooner he was got out of the way the better.

In principle the minute noted that approval for the project had been given by Foreign Secretary, Anthony Eden. Churchill's approval was confirmed with his initials 'WSC' written near Ismay's signature. Authority for the go-ahead of the assassination plan had been given from all concerned.[4]

When the bomb explodes inside the briefing hut in Hitler's Headquarters on 20th July, 1944, the initial thought among Hitler's entourage is that Allied bombers dropped it from the air. Only when Hitler's security men investigate the scene do they realise that the bomb actually had to have been planted inside the room rather than been dropped.

But the British plans, in June 1944, did indeed require low-flying bombing of a castle in Perpignan. Of course, Hitler never stayed or visited a castle in Perpignan, and the plan is abandoned, but it stimulates the SOE leadership into resuming an in-depth study how Hitler could be killed. The question of an assassination is raised again on 27th June 1944:

> *The points to be discussed will be how best to obtain knowledge of Hitler's movements, how to induce him, if necessary, to come to some locality at our investigation, how to deal with him there. At some time or other in the near future Hitler must in any case disappear from the scene, even if we should not be the direct agents for his elimination, and we can at least prepare such action to be taken on his disappearance as will contribute best towards the situation most favourable to the Allied Nations.[5]*

Even though some senior SOE members are personally against an assassination of Hitler because they believe that Nazi Germany's strategy and conduct of the war will most probably improve if Hitler is taken out of the equation. Especially the head of the German section, Section X, Lieutenant-Colonel Ronald Thornley believes that the German High Command would lead a more successful campaign, and that in the summer of 1944, it is Adolf Hitler's strategic incompetence which actually helps the Allied war efforts and the Allied advances on both fronts.[6] After lengthy internal discussions it is however decided that an SOE engineered assassination of Hitler is desirable, and in the event of being successful should be blamed

---

[4] D Rigden, op. cit., p. 50-51.
[5] Minute by Gubbins quoted in D Rigden, op. cit., p. 52.
[6] This opinion is also held by other senior military leaders, see A W Dulles, *Germany's Underground*, p. 145.

onto the German army to incite a 'clearly desirable civil war' inside Nazi Germany.[7]

A small task force is set into action to collect every piece of information on Hitler's movements, well-being, habits and any related matters which might aid an assassination plan. Copious detailed information is provided on Hitler's alpine retreat – the Berghof – in Berchtesgarden, and extensive documentary and photographic evidence is provided concerning his limousines and trains, including colour sketches of the uniforms worn by his guards.

The main thrust of the plans concentrates on Hitler's Berghof. When it comes to the recommended methods for an assassination attempt these consist of shooting the dictator by one of more snipers, a bazooka attack, or the poisoning of the water supply of the Führer, even poisoning the milk he allegedly likes to take with his tea. SOE also considers impregnating Hitler's clothes with lethal bacteria, and hide anthrax in a fountain pen. The option of explosives is also investigated, and one plan is to fling a suitcase full of explosives under Hitler's train as it passes through a railway station. Another – more outrageous plan – is to hypnotise Hitler's former deputy Rudolf Hess – who is in goal in Britain – into killing Hitler.[8]

The crucial problem of all these plans is: who would do 'the job' and how would they escape. Various groups are mentioned in the 'Operation Foxley' reports, potentially Czech or Polish resistance fighters, French forced labourers within Germany, or individually recruited SOE agents. But how would they get to Hitler's high security alpine retreat? And how would they make their escape?

Between July and November 1944 all sorts of various plans circulate among the SOE principals. Each of the various schemes to assassinate the dictator are re-examined – and in the end most of them rejected. One option is to send a first-class marksman to shoot Hitler from a distance during his constitutional walk from the Berghof to the tea-house, which is rejected as impracticable. Another plan to poison Hitler by poisoning the milk he takes with his tea, is rejected because it would entail poisoning a whole day's delivery. The proposal of 'doctoring' the drinking water in Hitler's personal train is rejected because SOE assumes that Hitler would be drinking

[7] SOE Meeting 28th June 1944, Gubbins, Lt.-Col. Ronald Thornley, Patrick Murray, Air Comm. Archibald Boyle, quoted in D Rigden, op. cit., p. 52-53.[8] See for more detailed descriptions of the plan, D Rigden, op. cit., chapters 5 and 6.

[8] See for more detailed descriptions of the plan, D Rigden, op. cit., chapters 5 and 6.

bottled water. The idea of using foreign cleaners to place a time-bomb on the Fuehrer's train is rejected because it is deemed impossible because it is assumed that Hitler's security would detect the bomb.[9]

As SOE plots how to kill the German dictator – there are concerns that German agents might plan to assassinate Churchill. MI5 is concerned that for example the Prime Minister's cigars could be poisoned. The consignments which are sent from Cuba and Brazil are under strict control but the

[9] D Rigden, op. cit., p. 57.
[10] M Gilbert, *Churchill*, p. 234.

Laventry Beria (left) and General Andrei Andreivich Vlassov.

PM often smokes them before they are being sent to MI5 for testing.[10]

Assassinating the enemy's leader is also a danger the Soviet leader, Josef Stalin, fears. His intelligence supremo, Lavrenty Beria, for instance, regularly updates and introduces new measures to increase the Soviet leader's security. But in the summer of 1944, Beria receives reports that Nazi Germany plans to carry out an assassination of the Soviet leader. According to these reports, a special Messerschmitt/Arado-332 is to drop a trained group of terrorists from Vlassov's Russian Army of Liberation, while other reports suggest that the Germans are going to leave a commando group behind enemy lines as they retreat, to assassinate Stalin.[11]

On 8th November, 1944, Section X of the SOE finally concludes that any assassination of Hitler is 'unsound and would not be in the interests of the Allied cause'. But the final report also reveals that 'among the highest in the land in England' there are 'several strong advocates' of the proposed assassination operation. It is tempting to speculate that Churchill is among these, bearing in mind his immediate

[11] D Volkogonov, *Stalin*, p. 480.
[12] D Rigden, op. cit., p. 59.

reaction to the proposed Perpignan plans and his frequent
strong support for bold and imaginative action.[12]

*Alan Welsh Dulles (left)
and Hans-Bernd
Gisevius*

The SOE plans are hampered with many ambiguities. But the
single biggest strategic flaw is that SOE never considered to
collaborate with the German resistance within Nazi Germany.
Surely it would have been easier for one of the German
resistance men in the military opposition to get closer to Hitler
than any foreign labourer. Another weakness is that all plans
focussed on Hitler's alpine retreat – a vast array of villas with an
equally high security surrounding them. It would have been
virtually impossible for any foreign agent to enter the Berghof
compound.

The beguiling question, could 'Operation Foxley' have worked,
has to be answered with an emphatic 'no'.

Yet, in the summer of 1944 – at the same time as SOE is
examining various possibilities of killing Adolf Hitler – the British
government has a very firm and distinctively different attitude to
the assassination attempts being harboured within Nazi Germany
against the German dictator.

The German opposition hopes by killing their enemy – Hitler –
they are also killing the Allies' enemy, and can become the Allies'

friend. But the situation in July 1944 is not as clear-cut as 'your enemy's enemy is your friend', as the renegade German generals are to find out.

The American deep-throat to the German opposition is a man called Allen Welsh Dulles.

Dulles became Chief of the New York Office of the Coordinator of information for the Office of Strategic Studies (OSS) – the predecessor to the CIA – in 1942 after the attack on Pearl Harbor and the German declaration of war against United States. In November of the same year, Dulles is posted as OSS station chief to Berne in Switzerland. He resides at Herrengasse 23, which borders a vineyard that enables his covert visitors to come and go unseen at night. His assignment above all is 'to find out what is going on in Germany'. Among other things – the standard sort of intelligence about armaments, supplies, morale, strategic intentions – the American government wanted to know 'who in Germany is really opposed to the Hitler régime and whether they are actively at work to overthrow it'.[13]

The sources for this sort of intelligence prove to be abundant in Switzerland. There are ordinary spies and traitors, exiles and expatriates, ecumenical church functionaries, businessmen, diplomats of neutral countries, and there are the opponents of the Hitler government.

Most of the reports Dulles and his staff file and send to OSS headquarters in Washington concern military matters, such as enemy formations, troop movements, bombing results and the German armaments industry. A substantial amount deals with the underground anti-Hitler movements in occupied France, Italy, the Balkans, Hungary and Austria – all of which receive Allied encouragement and material and ideological support.[14]

His best sources are German military-intelligence agents (*Abwehr*), among them it is Hans Bernd Gisevius who becomes Dulles' main contact. Gisevius, who serves as *Abwehr* agent in the German consulate in Zurich, argues vehemently for an arrangement between a German resistance government and the Western Allies to keep the Soviet Union out of Europe, and to prevent a co-operation between Hitler's Nazi successor and the Soviet Union. It is necessary, he informs Dulles in July 1944, to offer the resistance an alternative, a vision of a post-war Europe in which all nations, including a defeated Germany, can exist freely and in peace rather than make demands on the men of the German resistance 'which originate in the arsenal of the

---

[13] A W Dulles, *Germany's Underground*, p. XI.

[14] A W Dulles, op. cit., p. XVIII.

[15] A W Dulles, op. cit., p. XXII.

The British Foreign Minister, Anthony Eden.

anti-Hitler wartime propaganda'.[15] The German resistance hopes that the Western Allies will abandon their policy of 'unconditional surrender' towards Germany. While Dulles is stationed in Berne, he tries to influence the American policy in this direction.[16]

In his reports, Dulles informs Washington throughout 1944 – and ultimately London as these reports are shared – about the impending assassination attempt and the Generals plans to overthrow the Nazi regime.

In early April 1944, Dulles reports:

> *The German situation is rapidly approaching a climax. The end of the war in Europe is definitely in sight. In this crisis the resistance group in Germany state that they are now willing and ready to endeavour to initiate action for the removal of Hitler and the overthrow of the Nazis. ...The group is only prepared to proceed if they can get some reassurances from the Western powers that upon removal of the Nazis they can enter into direct negotiations with the Anglo-Saxons. ...After the overthrow of the Nazis, the German generals now in command at the Western Front would be prepared*

[16] A W Dulles, op. cit., p. 134.
[17] A W Dulles, op.cit., p. 136.

Clement Attlee

to give up resistance and to facilitate a landing of the Allied troops.[17]

The essence of the plan is, that the German army will open the way for the American and British troops to occupy Germany while the Russians are held at the Eastern Front. The resistance is encouraged to proceed by a most innocuous statement in the House of Commons by Clement Attlee on 6th July, 1944, to the general effect that before there could be any fresh consideration of the German situation the Germans themselves would have to take the first steps to rid themselves of their own criminal government. The German generals are also heartened by a statement of Winston Churchill at around the same time, in which he recommends the German people to overthrow the Nazi government.[18]

While the British government seems to encourage a coup within Germany – it is the crucial demand of 'unconditional

[18] A W Dulles, op. cit., p. 140.

surrender' that sits uneasy with their public statements. For the German opposition unconditional surrender to all three Allies – America, Britain and Soviet Union – means that they will be unable to counteract their enemy's slogan that the army is stabbing the nation and the fighting forces in the back by overthrowing Hitler.[19]

In early July Dulles reports from Berne take an ever more urgent tone:

> *Dramatic developments may be impending. Hope for full report tonight. Ruthless repression, is of course a possibility, even a probability!*[20]

This message of 12th July, 1944, is followed the next day with another:

> *The conspirators want to prove that Germans themselves can get rid of Hitler and his gang and establish a decent regime. The threat to German territory in the East and their desire to save as much of Germany as possible from Soviet occupation, has given the movement a new impetus. There will probably be an orderly withdrawal in the West if the plot succeeds.*[21]

Meanwhile in London the question of 'unconditional surrender' is being debated in the House of Commons on 18th July, 1944. The heated debate arises unexpectedly in the House on a routine motion for granting another £1,000,000,000 for the prosecution of the war, which is costing Britain between £11,000,000 and £13,000,000 million a day in July 1944. Prime Minister Churchill and Foreign Secretary Anthony Eden are criticized for insisting that Germany must surrender unconditionally. It is suggested in the House that the German people might overthrow their Nazi master sooner if the Allies can define now what they mean with these 'grim words'.[22]

Churchill is caught off guard with the ensuing heated exchanges in the House and the outspoken criticism of the Government's conduct of war. Under heavy V1 bombardment at home – 170,000 women and children need to be evacuated from London by the 20th July, 1944, – with the British invasion troops getting stuck around Caen in Northern France, and with an ever increasing war-debt. Parliament is getting more and more frustrated with the stated aim of the anti-Hitler coalition to make Germany surrender unconditionally. The growing discontent is voiced by the Rt Hon. Richard Stokes, who implies that the

[19] R Lamb, *Churchill*, p. 290.

[20] A W Dulles, op. cit., p. 140.

[21] A W Dulles, ibd.

[22] See New York Times, July 19th 1944, and R Lamb, op. cit., p. 288.

Government's avowed policy is prolonging rather than shortening the war:

> *All this is making our men face what they ought not be asked to face. The insistence on unconditional surrender, the threat to cut up German territory and cut off East Prussia, which Mr Churchill himself described as a purely German land with an intensely nationalistic population, can only make the Germans desperate.*[23]

Richard Stokes then questions Churchill on what was agreed in Teheran between the three Allied leaders. Explicitly he asks whether it had been decided to give East Prussia to the Soviet Union, to which Churchill replies that these things should only be discussed around a peace table.[24]

Clearly, Britain is unable to support or welcome the German army coup against Hitler officially. Within the greater scheme of the anti-Hitler coalition, the renegade German generals attempt to change the course of the war and to change the régime was futile to start with.

It seems that after the war, however, Winston Churchill regretted his intransigence and refusal to countenance talks with the dissidents within Nazi Germany. The question remains, whether Churchill did throw away an opportunity to end the war in July 1944. He was always frightened that unilateral negotiations, without the Soviets, might edge Stalin into a separate peace with Hitler. In addition with memories of the Cabinet at the time at Dunkirk Churchill feared that peace talks might destroy the British nation's will to fight.

After the war Churchill claims that he had been misled by his assistants about the considerable strength and size of the anti-Hitler resistance,

> *...in Germany there lived an opposition which was weakened by their losses and an enervating international policy, but which belongs to the noblest and greatest that the political history of any nation has ever produced. These men fought without help from within or from abroad – driven forward only by the restlessness of their conscience. As long as they lived they were invisible and unrecognisable to us, because they had to camouflage themselves. But their death made their resistance visible.*[25]

However, on the 22nd July, 1944, two days after the failed Stauffenberg assassination attempt, the BBC broadcasts a report which named conspirators of the coup who had not yet been arrested by the Gestapo. The broadcast was written by Maurice

[23] R Stokes in the House of Commons, 18th July 1944.
[24] New York Times, 19th July 1944.
[25] W Churchill, quoted in R Lamb, op. cit., p. 292. [26] N Bird in Letters to the Editor, The Times, 13th July 1996.

Entrance to the BBC's Broadcasting House.

Latey of the BBC's German Service at the request of Hugh Greene, its editor. Greene had received a tape carrying a long list of names of those believed to be implicated in the coup against Hitler, from which Latey extracted the most important ones. The tape had been sent by the Political Warfare Executive (PWE), based at Woburn Abbey, who were responsible for the policy of broadcasts in German. Whether the publication of these names via a BBC broadcast in July 1944 was authorised or simply a mistake is still unclear.[26]

Even though no direct links can be made – it seems that the spirit of the BBC broadcast is reflected in a memorandum written by John Wheeler-Bennett, who was the deputy to Bruce Lockhart, the head of the Political PWE of the Foreign Office.

On 25th July, 1944 – five days after the Stauffenberg attempt – Wheeler-Bennett sends the following memorandum to Prime Minister Churchill and Foreign Secretary Anthony Eden:

> *It may now be said with some definitiveness that we are better off with things as they stand today than if the plot of the 20th July had succeeded and Hitler had been assassinated. In this event the 'Old Army' Generals would have taken over ...and put into operation a peace move already prepared in which Germany would admit defeat herself and sue for terms other than Unconditional Surrender. In the failure of the plot we have been spared the embarrassment both at*

[26] N Bird in Letters to the Editor, The Times, 13th July 1996.

*home and in the United States which might have resulted from such
a move, and moreover the present purge is presumably removing from
the scene numerous individuals who might have caused us difficulty
not only had the plot succeeded, but also after a defeat of Nazi
Germany. ...the Gestapo and SS have done us an appreciable service
in removing a selection of those who would undoubtedly have posed
as 'good Germans' after the war while preparing for a Third World
War. It is to our advantage therefore that the purge should continue
since the killing of Germans by Germans will save us from future
embarrassments.*[27]

Churchill accepts Wheeler-Bennett's evaluation of the situation
for his statement in the House of Commons on the 12th August,
1944, when he says:

*The highest personalities in the Reich are murdering one another or
trying to, while the avenging armies of the Allies close upon the doomed
and ever-narrowing circle of their power.*[28]

But there are also voices of opposition in the House:

*Now we know there is a strong element in the German army which
thinks that continuance of the war is foolish and suicidal, we should
change our whole policy. How can one expect a movement of that sort
to be widespread and broad-based if the Germans have nothing to go
on except the repeated cry of 'unconditional surrender', and daily
statements by Dr Goebbels telling the people that if Germany is
conquered we are going to cut Germany up and do awful things to its
men and women.*[29]

Unconditional surrender – the cornerstone of the Anglo-
American alliance – is not only criticised in the British Parliament.
Several months earlier, as soon as Eisenhower took command of
the invasion forces in January 1944, he demands that he should
be allowed to present more attractive propositions to the German
armed forces. For the military man Eisenhower unconditional
surrender means that German forces are going to fight to the
bitter end, rather than surrender when the battle-situation clearly
shows that they are defeated.[30]

But even Eisenhower has to accept, that unconditional
surrender is a pre-condition for peace.

As regional commanders across Nazi Germany – from Paris to
Prague – side with the renegade Generals in Berlin on this fateful

---

[27] J Wheeler-Bennett, 25th July 1944 memorandum, quoted in R Lamb, op. cit., p. 292.

[28] R Lamb, op. cit., p. 292.

[29] George Strauss in the House of Commons 12th August 1944, quoted in R Lamb, op.
cit., p. 293.

[30] R Lamb, op. cit., p. 294.

20th July, 1944 – it is clear to Winston Churchill as he receives   *Franklin D Roosevelt*
intelligence reports about the uprising in Germany that this might   *with Winston Churchill*
completely unbalance the fragile alliance between himself,
Roosevelt and Stalin.

If the renegade German generals are successful and
overthrow the Nazi régime their actions will put Churchill
under enormous pressure at home to accept their surrender.
However, his close war-time ally and major creditor, President
Roosevelt, has made clear that unconditional surrender is non-
negotiable. Their Soviet ally has two options: either offer
conditional surrender to Germany or side with Roosevelt and
press for a continuation of the war until unconditional
surrender on all fronts is achieved.

As the 20th July, 1944, comes to a close it will become clear
that the plot to kill Hitler and to end the Nazi régime has failed.
And the reality of war means that the men – and women – who
fought against Hitler from within Nazi Germany are not
welcome.

For Churchill it is time to prepare for his evening briefings
with his Chiefs of Staff – and to pack for his impending journey
to Normandy. He is the only war leader who actively seeks to
visit the troops near the frontline – to give encouragement and
support – often driving his commanders to despair – as they
have to cater for the special security measures for their Prime
Minister.

CHAPTER ELEVEN

2000 Hours – San Diego

To Win the War

What is the job before us in 1944? First to win the war – to win the war fast, to win it overwhelmingly.

FDR acceptance speech, 20th July, 1944

THURSDAY, 20th July, 1944 – the presidential train is parked in a siding in the yards of San Diego. Tomorrow, FDR will embark on his sea voyage to Hawaii to meet with General MacArthur and Admiral Nimitz.

His trip to San Diego is an official secret. The President's secret service agents have tried to keep the President's whereabouts hidden from the American public. The train journey has no scheduled stops and no crowds are being addressed. At each engineering stop, the President and his party are asked to stay aboard the train. But FDR's famous Scottie dog, Fala, has to be taken off to relieve himself. When Pullman porters and ticket takers see Fala, they know who really is aboard the train, called 'Main 985'.[1]

FDR sits in the observation car revising his acceptance speech, as the Democratic convention delegates in Chicago are going through the motions of nominating him for a fourth term. It is late afternoon in San Diego, and a telegram arrives from the Convention Chairman, Senator Jackson, informing FDR officially that he has been named as Democratic nominee for President. The final tally is Roosevelt 1,086 against Harry Bird of Virginia 89 votes.

In effect, Roosevelt's nomination is a foregone conclusion. No other candidate unites the Democratic Party as much as the wartime President. The question however is, whether the delegates would have nominated him, had they known how ill their President really is. Only hours ago, he was lying helplessly on the floor, struck by an attack.

[1] M Beschloss, *The Conquerors*, p. 5.

The President's resident cardiologist, Dr Howard Bruenn, concluded earlier that FDR was in cardiac failure with a grossly enlarged heart and a tortuous aorta. Bruenn later recalled that he was appalled that the President ran for a fourth term. Modern anti-hypertensive drugs could have relieved the burden on Roosevelt's arteries, but those didn't exist in 1944. Bruenn recalled that there was little he could do but 'protect him from stress, keep down his excitement, insist on him having rest after

The launching of a V2 rocket.

lunch, cutting back on his smoking to six cigarettes a day and reducing his weight'. After obstinately obeying Bruenn's rigid diet, Roosevelt loses more than twenty pounds, which leaves him looking gaunt and hollow-cheeked.[2]

The President struggles with the final wording for his acceptance speech. Writing and delivering speeches – formerly a joy for FDR – has now become a burden. Tonight's speech, which will be broadcast to the Democratic Convention assembled in Chicago by radio, has taken the better part of the last six days to finesse. It has taken his trusted secretary Grace Tully the past two days to redraft and retype it. Dr Bruenn's strict health régime means that FDR can't find solace in his beloved Martini cocktails before dinnertime.[3] His female companion Daisy Stuckley complains:

> *Everyone with high blood pressure I ever heard of has always been deprived of all stimulants![4]*

The lack of stimulants is however one of the President's least problem. In the European theatre of war, his close wartime ally, Prime Minister Winston Churchill, faces public criticism for the British government's helplessness in the face of Nazi-Germany's terror weapons. Churchill has indicated that before relief might be obtained even worse can be expected.

And as the British civilian casualties population again suffers the brunt of Hitler's air warfare – it is American military planners who suspect that the new weapons being developed in Nazi Germany eventually might reach the American continent. The Allies are aware that the V1 weapons are just the beginning and that the next generation of V2s is just around the corner. These, the Allies knew, were rocket propelled, able to cover longer distances, and could potentially be launched from German U-boats close to the American coastline.

A yet more dreaded possibility in the summer of 1944 is that Nazi Germany might make progress on their own version of the 'Tube Alloys' – the Allied codename for the Atomic Weapons Manhattan Project at Los Alamos. Germany had once been world leader in the field of experimental nuclear physics under Werner von Heisenberg. His former scientist colleagues, now emigrated and living in America and Britain, fear that Nazi Germany has made further advances in this direction. Hitler's continued referring to the new 'miracle weapons' which were being developed in Nazi Germany and would soon bring the turning

[2] M Beschloss, op. cit., p. 83.

[3] R Ferrell, *The Dying President*, p. 74.

[4] R Ferrell, op. cit., p. 76.

*The rear carriage of
FDR's train 'Ferdinand
Magellan'.*

point in the war, lead many to believe that this refers to a German Atom Bomb.[5]

In the Pacific, the Japanese Tojo Cabinet has resigned, because the Emperor is 'distressed' over Japan's position after having lost Saipan to the Americans. The new government is headed by General Koiso, known as the 'Tiger of Korea', a tough man, whose job it is to add his toughness to the Japanese war effort. Even though American forces are progressing – it does mean that more bloody battles will follow.

This is the backdrop of the global picture of war on Thursday, 20th July, 1944, the day that FDR accepts his re-nomination.

It is 1900 hours and FDR entertains his two sons and his daughters-in-law in his private car. After dinner the party moves back to the observation car.[6] He is joined by his speech writer, Sam Rosenman, his military advisor, Admiral William Leahy, and his cardiologist Dr Bruenn.

Sitting at a small desk, FDR delivers his acceptance speech at 2020hours, the radio announcer introduces the old and new presidential candidate as 'speaking from the Pacific Coast Naval base' – his voice comes booming out. The speech is broadcast live into the Convention Hall, where the spotlights focus on a huge photograph of the President.

[5] J Black, *World War Two*, p. 181-182.
[6] FDR Day by Day The Pare Lorentz Chronology, Grace Tully's Appointment Diary entry

In his speech, Roosevelt defends his war record, castigates doubters and opponents, and speaks in broad but not specific terms about his vision of a fourth term. What he has to say is tactful rather than statesmanlike. He reiterates his desire to retire to 'the quiet life', but 'you in this convention have asked me to continue'. FDR acknowledges that he will be 'too busy to campaign in the usual sense' and 'he hopes for re-election as President on the basis of maturity versus immaturity', an unveiled stab at the relative youth of his most likely Republican opponent, Thomas D Dewey, and his criticism, that 'old senile men' are governing the country from the White House.

For those voters who might waver between Roosevelt and Dewey, he has a special caution: It will be up to them to decide in November 1944, whether plans already made and the men already serving to achieve victory, will make the world a better place, or whether a new administration with no program except to 'oppose' would achieve this aim.[7]

FDR addressing the 1944 Democratic Convention.

But it is the war which dominates FDR's acceptance speech:

[7] J Bishop, *FDR's Last Year*, p. 108.

It seems wholly likely that within the next four years our armed forces and those of our Allies will have gained a complete victory over Germany and Japan, and that the world will once again be at peace...

The wartime President then outlines his vision for the immediate and the long-term future:

What is the job before us in 1944? First to win the war – to win the war fast, to win it overwhelmingly. Second, to form worldwide international organisations – and third, to build an economy for our returning veterans and for all Americans – which will provide employment and decent standard of living.[8]

At the end of his speech there is thunderous applause in the Convention Hall. The huge photo of the President in the hall shows a healthy and smiling President. FDR is re-nominated.

Franklin D Roosevelt has tried to give his voice a freshness of purpose. It is fortunate, that the delegates only hear his voice and don't see the President as he really looks. How far his health has deteriorated is, however, revealed to the nation as a whole in a press photo by Associated Press, which is published the next day in newspapers all over America. It is a photo that shocks a nation, who hasn't seen him for the past half year, and is a first sign of the failing health of their President.

The photo depicts FDR during the transmission of his speech. FDR sits at a small table in the observation car, looking haggard. The eyes are dark sockets. The thin shoulders sag in an oversized jacket. The small table reveals the President's thin, withered legs, and the wide trousers of the time accentuated them. He is reading his address, and his face is turned down, hence elongated, which makes him look even more unwell. He has his mouth open, the photograph catches him speaking, which gives him the appearance of being unable to control his facial muscles and perhaps having suffered from some sort of stroke. It is at this point that the people, rather than the politicians, begin to think of their President as a sick man.

The photograph bothers Press Secretary Early, who writes to FDR's secretary Grace Tully, and shows how far spin has entered US politics already in 1944:

I was terrifically disappointed ...when I saw the photograph of the President delivering his speech of acceptance. I have not seen the newsreels but I hope they are better than the stills... I suggest that any further pictures are postponed until the President has had a good night's sleep. The rumour factory is working overtime – making all it can out

---

[8] Presidential Speeches, Transcripts, FDR Library, 20th July 1944.

of the photograph.[9]

As soon as the President's speech concludes and the applause for Roosevelt subsides in the Chicago Convention Hall, the arena erupts into a violent pro-Wallace demonstration. 30,000 unauthorised people on the floor and in the galleries start holding up placards and start chanting 'We want Wallace. We want Wallace'. At this fever-pitched moment, the Democratic Party bosses start to panic.

Wallace supporters want to hijack the euphoria of FDR's acceptance speech to push for an automatic nomination of the sitting Vice-President, Henry Wallace, on the same night. What ensues is mayhem. In their desperation to stop the motion to nominate Wallace, party officials around Bob Hannegan decide to dissolve and adjourn the meeting. They call on Mayor Kelly to give them a good reason to stop the session, who dissolves the meeting under the fire laws.

The Wallace supporters are furious, fire axes are drawn and the exit doors flung open. Outside thousands of citizens try to force their way in as the delegates and the Wallace supporters crash outwards. Ribs begin to crack; women faint; snake dancers walk over fallen persons; and Senator Jackson hangs on a gavel and

The convention audience during FDR's speech.

[9] R Ferrell, op. cit., p. 79.

shouts 'Session adjourned'. But no one hears him.[10]

The next day, Friday, 21st July, 1944, party boss Hannegan has Harry S Truman in Room H under the stands, shaking hands with delegates he has never met. While up on the convention floor Henry Wallace walks the aisles, shaking hands, grinning, asking for votes. Finally, the chairman starts the roll call.

The first ballot ends with Wallace at 429 to Truman's 319. But the second sees a reversal of fortunes for Truman: with 1,031 votes against 105 for Wallace, Harry S Truman is nominated as FDR's running mate for the 1944 elections.[11]

Getting the relatively unknown Truman on the ticket is a major achievement for the lobbying of Bob Hannegan's 'harmony boys'. But it does mean that FDR has surrendered the New Deal. Opting for the compromise candidate Truman sends a signal to the Southern Democrats that the civil rights agenda of the Democratic Party, is for the moment, put on hold. In

FDR broadcasting his speech to the convention.

[10] J Bishop, op. cit., p. 109.
[11] J Bishop, op. cit., p. 110.

effect it means that the great sacrifice of American black soldiers in the Second World War will only be honoured much later in the civil rights legislation under the Kennedy and Lyndon B Johnson administrations.

Harry S Truman will turn out to be a very decisive President. It is hard to imagine that Henry Wallace would have reacted in the same dramatic manner as Truman in concluding the Second World War. It is hard to conceive that Wallace, the arm-chair intellectual would have sanctioned the use of the Atomic Bombs. Truman's upfront, dry prairie style personality shaped decisive confrontations with the American labour movement and new enemies in the emerging Cold War. Post-war American history would have been different, if on the evening of the 20th July, 1944, the Wallace supporters would have got their way and had forced a Wallace nomination.[12]

For the time, however, it is President Roosevelt who dominates the war effort, and some critics say, that FDR should probably have had a rest and engineered a proper hand-over to Truman.

Vice President Harry S Truman with President Franklin D Roosevelt.

[12] M Beschloss, op. cit., p. 54.

But FDR had grown too accustomed to the job and the power, to let go. In terms of the ongoing strategy during the war, critics say that had he been at the height of his physical strength, he would have fought and negotiated harder with the Soviet leader Stalin during the crucial months of Soviet military advances into Central Europe.

Thursday 20th July 1944, it is a warm summer evening in Kuntsevo, at Marshal Stalin's dacha near Moscow. Winning the war is also Stalin's key aim. The Soviet dictator is relaxing in the dacha's garden:

> *He loved the garden, the flowers and the woods that were all around, they were my father's hobby and relaxation. He never dug the earth or took a shovel in his hand the way real gardeners do. But he liked things to be cultivated and kept up. He liked the blossoms to be abundant. He liked to see the ripe cherries, apples and tomatoes. ...In the summer he spent days in the garden, he had his official papers, news papers and tea brought to him in the park.*[13]

Eastern and Central Europe is foremost on Stalin's mind. More precisely: Poland.

Stalin's first objective, as the German troops retreat in summer 1944, is to recover permanently for the Soviet Union the territories which he had secured previously in the Hitler-Stalin Pact. In Stalin's view, the two Western Allies, Roosevelt and Churchill, have already agreed – indeed suggested it to him in Teheran – that the new Soviet-Polish frontier should follow the line agreed with Hitler, dressed up for the sake of respectability as the so-called Curzon-Line, with compensation in the West at Germany's expense. This is going to be the first and most difficult part of the post-war settlement, and is going to create unrelieved tragedy. In essence, Stalin aims to carve up Poland and move his western borders considerably west-ward. The injustice of the Hitler-Stalin Pact is to continue.[14]

2200 hours – Stalin is now inside the dacha.

> *My father lived in one room, in fact, and made it do everything for him. He slept on the sofa, made up at night as a bed, and had telephones on the table beside him. The large dining table was piled high with official papers, newspapers and books. He used one end for eating, the other for working.*[15]

He is pacing up and down, smoking continuously his beloved

---

[13] Recollections of Stalin's daughter Svetlana, in: S Alliluyeva, *20 Letters to a friend*, p. 124.
[14] A Bullock, *Hitler and Stalin*, p. 939.
[15] S Alluyeva, op. cit., p. 137.

Reconstruction of Stalin receiving the news of the attempted assassination of Hitler.

American cigarettes, while being briefed by his Chief-of-Staff, General Alexei Antonov, in the so-called 'night report'. Having surrounded himself with superb staff officers, as well as exceptional field commanders, who are in constant contact with the Soviet leader, Stalin nevertheless has to approve all operational and strategic decisions, and insists on face-to-face reports by his senior military advisors. All relevant material has been carefully sorted and filed in advance. Three files are being used during the briefings:

> *Top-priority documents, which were reported first, went into a red folder. Most of these were orders, directives, instructions, and arms distribution plans for the army in the field and the reserves. A blue folder was kept for papers of secondary importance, usually various requests which were dealt with selectively, as far as possible, but usually every day. ...The green folder contained recommendations*

for promotion and decorations, and proposals and orders concerning appointments and re-appointments ...dealt with only in favourable instances.[16]

Among the papers in Antonov's red folder on this 20th July, 1944, is Stalin's instruction to the Red Army in the field that a Polish Committee for National Liberation is to be set up to establish Soviet control over Poland. In only two days the Committee is declared the new provisional government of Poland. It is hand-picked by Stalin. The same day, the 22nd July, 1944, this Lublin Government signs an agreement with the Soviet Union at a ceremony which is attended by Stalin. The fate of post-war Poland is sealed.

Unlike the Eastern European nations from whom Stalin claims territory, the Poles alone fought the Germans and have suffered terribly at their hands. They never collaborated with them or sent troops to join the Germans attacking the Soviet Union in 1941. But none of this weighs with Stalin. He already seized the opportunity of the Katyn Affair[17] to break off relations with the exiled Polish government in London. Stalin also refuses to recognize the Polish Home Army, who fights bravely against the Nazi occupiers.

Not only does Stalin refuse to accept the Polish resistance fighters, he actively destroys them. Once a Polish area is liberated from the Nazis by the Red Army, the Soviet security forces arrest, frequently on charges of 'collaboration with the Germans', any Pole who refuses to accept the Soviet authority.

Only one day after the Soviet-style Polish puppet régime is installed, the Red Army liberates one of the first Nazi extermination camps in occupied Poland, Majdanek. In a terrible irony of history, the first new inmates in this camp will be the Polish resistance members who refuse to accept 'their' new government.[18]

For Stalin the war means a true reversal of fortunes and an impressive enlargement of his territory and spheres of influence in Eastern Europe. This is not something he wants to discuss with his other Allies, when the war is going well for him. Stalin knows that especially the British Prime Minister is infuriated by his actions in Poland.

Churchill is desperate to have another meeting of the Big Three Allies to discuss post-war settlements, especially what happens to

[16] S M Shtemenko, *The Soviet General Staff at war 1941-1945*, p. 137, p. 119.

[17] In 1940 on Stalin's orders, the NKVD shot and buried over 4000 Polish service personnel that had been taken prisoner when the Soviet Union invaded Poland in September 1939 in WW2 in support of the Nazis.

[18] A Bullock, op. cit., p. 941.

Reconstruction of Stalin in conference.

the territories in Eastern Europe, which the Soviet Union is liberating.

Knowing Churchill's wish to meet, Roosevelt dispatches a telegram to Stalin. If the cable is politically motivated it is poorly conceived, but on the other hand if it is designed to spare Poland – which is doubtful – it is surely too late:

Number 27. Top Secret and Personal

From the President to Josef Stalin

> *Things are moving so fast and so successfully that I feel there should be a meeting between you and Mr Churchill and me in the reasonably near future. The Prime Minister is in hearty accord with this thought. I am now on a trip in the Far West and must be in Washington for several weeks on my return. It would therefore be best for me to have a meeting between the tenth and the fifteenth of September. The most central point for you and me would be the North of Scotland. I could go by ship you could come either by ship or by plane. I hope you can let me have your thoughts. Secrecy and security can be maintained either aboard a ship or on shore. Roosevelt.*[19]

Meeting Roosevelt and Churchill is far from desirable to Stalin. Moreover, he is somewhat of a 'homebody', and what is little

[19] J Bishop, *FDR's last year*, p. 107.

known, actually afraid of flying. But most of all, the timing for such a meeting is crucial, and the later it takes place, the better for Stalin.[20] His reply to Roosevelt is therefore:

> *Such a meeting will not be feasible. When the Soviet armies are involved in battles on such a wide front, as they are now, it would be impossible for me to leave the country. All my colleagues consider it absolutely impossible.*[21]

Stalin is not willing to give up the advantage he has in July 1944. The Three Allies will only meet in Yalta in February 1945, which will be their last meeting.

As General Antonov finishes his report and the day comes to a close in Kuntsevo, Stalin asks his housekeeper Valetchka to start serving his dinner. It was a good days work, the war is going Stalin's way.

[20] H Hyde, *Stalin*, p. 452.
[21] H Hyde, op. cit., p. 459.

CHAPTER TWELVE

0000 Hours – Berlin

Long Live Sacred Germany

Lang lebe das Heilige Deutschland!

Stauffenberg before the execution squad.

I N the Wolf's Lair, deep in the East-Prussian forest, Hitler now knows that a considerable part of the German army has plotted to kill him and to overthrow his régime. Being far away from the German capital Berlin, Hitler fears that the revolt might still spread.

At around 1900hours a telephone call is put through from Berlin. It is Propaganda Minister Joseph Goebbels. He tells Hitler that a Major Ernst Remer is with him and has orders to arrest Goebbels. Remer has received his orders from the renegade Generals. As a fanatical Hitler-loyalist, Remer initially believes the plotters story that the SS is behind the attempt on the Führer. Confronted by Goebbels, who insists that Hitler is alive, Remer waivers.[1]

In one of the most surreal events of this fateful 20th July 1944, Goebbels hands the telephone receiver to Major Remer. Hitler, with his ears deafened by the bomb, can hardly hear the answers on the other end of the line, and shouts down the receiver:

Major Remer, do you recognise my voice? They tried to kill me, but I am alive. I am speaking to you as your Supreme Commander. Only my orders are to be obeyed. You are to restore order in Berlin for me. Use whatever force you consider necessary. Shoot anybody who tries to disobey my orders.[2]

Major Remer is the commander of the Berlin City Battalion. Only half an hour ago, he and his men had set out to arrest Propaganda Minister Goebbels as one of the 'ringleaders' of the conspiracy against Hitler. Now, he returns to the German Army Headquarter in the Bendlerstrasse, his orders have turned 360 degrees. He is ordered to arrest the 'real' conspirators, Colonel Stauffenberg and his associates. The time is up for the army rebellion.

At Hitler's Headquarters in East-Prussia meanwhile the

---

[1] N v Below, *At Hitler's Side*, p. 210-211.
[2] I Kershaw, *Hitler 1936-1945 Nemesis*, p. 680.

Reconstruction of Remer talking to Hitler in Geobbel's office.

injuries begin to tell on Hitler's physique. At 2000hours, Hitler's personal physician Dr Theodore Morell checks Hitler's pulse again: it is now 100, and he treats the injuries with his own 'penicillin' powder, which in fact is quite useless, if not actually toxic, and dictates his medical notes to his typist:

> *Right forearm badly swollen, prescribed acid aluminium acetate compresses. Effusion of blood on right shinbone has subsided. On back of third and fourth finger of left hand there is a large burn blister. Dressed this. Occiput partly and hair completely singed, a palm-sized second degree burn on the middle of the calf and a number of contusions and open flesh wounds. Left forearm has effusion of blood on interior aspect and is badly swollen, can move only with difficulty. Told him to take two Optalidons[3] and two table-spoons of Brom-Nervacit[4] before going to sleep.[5]*

The assassin's bomb affects Hitler more than he likes to admit. The next day, on 21st July, 1944, he starts to suffer violent ear pains, and his right ear begins to bleed continuously. His eyes constantly flick to the right (nystagmus). Alone in his bunker, he keeps thinking that he is falling over to the right. During the evening, as he goes for a short walk in the twilight, he finds himself twice wandering off the path. He has a constant taste of blood in his mouth. Dr Erwin Giesing, an ear-nose-and-throat expert is called in on 22nd July, 1944 and Hitler confesses to him that he can't sleep despite Dr Morell's Phanodorm sleeping tablets. Giesing notices that Hitler's voice is unnaturally loud, and that the Führer is lip reading other people's replies. Another day passes, and on 23rd July another

[3] An analgesic.
[4] A tranquiliser.
[5] D Irving, *The Secret Diaries of Hitler's Doctor*, p. 187.

specialist is brought in, Dr Carl von Eicken – who operated on Hitler's vocal cords in 1935 – to find out why the ear is still bleeding despite the hemostatic pills and injections, which Dr Morell keeps administering.[6]

But on the 20th July 1944, his miraculous survival invigorates Hitler. Dining that evening with his secretaries, Hitler voices his anger at the assassins:

> *What cowards! If they had drawn a gun on me, I might still respect them. But they didn't dare risk their own lives! ...Traitors. They deserve the most ignominious of deaths, ...exterminate them. Put their wives and children into concentration camps and show them no mercy.*[7]

Allegedly, he even confronts his Alsatian dog:

> *Look me in the eyes Blondi. Are you a traitor like the generals?*[8]

As Hitler builds up more and more revenge thoughts and prepares his speech to the German nation, the plotters turn on themselves in Berlin.

Colonel Stauffenberg stubbornly refuses to give up:

> *The fellow isn't dead after all, but the machine is running, one can't say yet how it will go.*[9]

While his heroism is admirable, his failure to accept the

Hitler nursing his injured right arm with General Jodl who sustained head injuries.

[6] F Redlich, *Hitler*, p. 286.

[7] T Junge, *Bis zur letzten Stunde*, p. 150.

[8] M Beschloss, *The Conquerors*, p. 3.

[9] P Hoffmann, *Stauffenberg*, p. 273-274.

realities of the failed coup is incomprehensible: Neither the
government quarter, nor the radio stations have been brought
under the conspirators' control; nor are there any battle-ready
units standing by. Stauffenberg badly misjudges the events. At
around 2000hours Stauffenberg tells the commander of Army
Group North, Major-General Kinzel, that contrary to the radio
broadcast, he knew for sure that the truth was that Hitler was
dead, and that the army had taken over. Several senior army
officers now arrive at the Army Headquarters. Field Marshal
von Witzleben among them demands that Stauffenberg explain
himself. When Stauffenberg reports to him, Witzleben does not
believe him, and concludes with the typical no-nonsense
attitude of a Prussian general: 'A fine mess this is'.[10]

Witzleben (left) and Beck.

After Witzleben has left, Stauffenberg hurries back to the
telephones, shouting encouragement to his fellow conspirators
with a fervour born out of desperation. Even he must sense the
growing coolness and distance on all sides. Everywhere there are
signs that the Nazis are gaining the upper hand again. The City
Battalion Commander, Major Remer, has defected, and several
other army heads are declaring their loyalty to the Führer.

As news of Hitler's survival spreads through the various

[10] P Hofmann, op. cit., p. 275.

offices and along the corridors at the German Army Headquarters in Bendlerstrasse, loyalists and opportunists now try to contain the damage of the actions of the renegade officers. Everyone passing through the corridors is confronted at gunpoint with the question 'Are you for or against the Führer?' It is shortly after 2300 hours on 20th July, 1944.[11]

Stauffenberg's superior, General Fromm, until now under arrest in an office, realizes that the backdoor has been left unguarded, and succeeds in contacting the branch heads of the reserve army, ordering countermeasures. He is released by other loyal fellow officers, who start disarming the conspirators. Together they confront Stauffenberg and the leaders of the army rebellion with drawn pistols. Fromm remarks: 'So, gentlemen, now it's my turn to do to you what you did to me this afternoon.'[12]

Major Otto-Ernst Remer.

[11] J Fest, *Plotting Hitler's death*, p. 273, p. 276.
[12] J Fest, op. cit., p. 276.

Fromm pronounces that they have been caught in the act of high treason, declares them arrested and demands their weapons.[13]

The most senior of the conspirators, General Ludwig Beck, asks to keep his pistol in order to shoot himself. Wishing to make a final statement, Fromm replies gruffly: 'Go ahead, but be quick about it!' Beck raises his revolver to his temple and begins with his speech, but Fromm cuts him off impatiently. Beck pauses and then in front of the others, squeezes the trigger. The bullet merely grazes his head. Fromm orders two officers to take his revolver away, but Beck resists clumsily, firing and wounding himself a second time, collapsing in a heap – still alive. Leaving the former Chief of General Staff dying on the floor, Fromm grants the other conspirators a moment to write a statement.[14]

News reaches Fromm that SS-Chief Heinrich Himmler and SS troops are on their way to arrest the army conspirators. Having played a double-game until now, and as superior to

[13] P Hoffmann, op. cit., p. 277.
[14] Ibid.

Stauffenberg neither supporting nor actively opposing the renegade officers during the planning of their plot, Fromm needs to save his neck, and decides to execute the main conspirators himself, before the SS arrives.[15]

> *In the name of the Führer, I have convened a court-martial that has pronounced the following sentence: General Staff Colonel Mertz von Quirnheim, General Olbricht, the colonel whose name I will not speak, and Lieutenant Haeften are condemned to death. Take a few men and execute the sentence downstairs in the courtyard at once.*[16]

Stauffenberg tries to take all the responsibility on his own shoulders, claiming in a few clipped sentences that the others had acted purely as soldiers and his subordinates, following his orders.

Glancing down at Beck, who is still in his death throes, Fromm orders an officer standing nearby to put him out of his misery, but the officer refuses, protesting that this is not worthy of such an esteemed General. A staff sergeant is finally ordered to kill the General. He drags Beck into an adjoining room, where he is unceremoniously shot in the head.[17]

It is just after midnight on 20th July, 1944.

Four men are escorted down the stairs and into the courtyard of the German Army Headquarters in the Bendlerstrasse.[18]

Several army trucks have been pulled up, their headlights glaring. The drivers have been ordered to turn their headlights on a little pile of sandbags near the doorway to the courtyard. Along all sides of the square, groups of curious onlookers are gathering. In the middle stands the execution squad consisting of Lieutenant Werner Schady, and ten non-commissioned officers of the Berlin city guard-battalion.

As the four conspirators emerge from the staircase, they are positioned in front of the small pile of sandbags. Without ceremony, the first, Lieutenant-General Friedrich Olbricht, is promptly shot. Then it's Stauffenberg's turn. But just as the squad fires, his Lieutenant Werner von Haeften, in a defiant gesture, throws himself into the bullets destined for his friend and superior.

His noble gesture is to no avail. Stauffenberg is immediately placed in front of the pile again. When the squad takes aim again at Stauffenberg, he shouts putting Germany before Hitler: Long live sacred Germany!

Seconds later, the firing squad takes aim again and executes the fourth conspirator Colonel Mertz von Quirnheim.

[15] J Fest, op. cit., p. 277.

[16] I Kershaw, op. cit., p. 682.

[17] J Fest, op. cit., p. 277.; I Kershaw, op. cit., p. 682.

[18] See for description of the execution: J Fest, op. cit., p. 275-279; I Kershaw, op. cit., p. 682-683; and P Hoffmann, op. cit., p. 276-277.

Almost immediately, General Fromm dispatches a telegram to the Führer Headquarters in East Prussia, claiming that he suppressed the rebellion and executed the ringleaders. He then addresses the men assembled in the courtyard, attributing Hitler's miraculous survival and salvation to the work of Providence. He ends his speech with a three-fold '*Sieg Heil*' to the Führer. Onlookers and soldiers enthusiastically join in.[19] The remaining conspirators in the Bendlerstrasse, among them Stauffenberg's brother Berthold, are arrested.

General Beck's bloody body is dragged down the staircase and thrown together with the other bodies onto an army truck. All of them are carted away to the nearby cemetery of St Matthew's Church in the Tiergarten. The custodian is instructed to inter the bodies – with their uniforms and decorations – secretly that very night.

Satisfied with himself and convinced that at the end of a long and confusing day, he managed 'to come down on the right side', General Fromm makes his way to Propaganda Minister Goebbels. He wants to be the first to report in person that the conspiracy has been crushed. Then perhaps he will be able to speak to Hitler himself. But Fromm's frantic covering of his tracks, is seen as the opportunism it is, and upon arrival at Goebbel's office, he is immediately arrested. He will be executed in March 1945.

On the evening when the conspiracy of the renegade German generals comes to a macabre end in a courtyard in Berlin, it is Allen Dulles, the man who until now has informed the Western

Claus von Stauffenberg and Mertz von Quirnheim taken before Stauffenberg's injuries.

Allies about the impending army rebellion, who calls his superiors at the Office of Strategic Services (OSS) headquarters in Washington by radiophone. The tone of his message is sober:

> *The attempt on Hitler's life is of course, the outstanding item of the news this evening. ...The man seems to have a charmed life, but possibly an all-wise Providence is saving him so that he may himself see the complete wreckage of the Germany he has led to destruction. ...I presume you all have the news we have on this – we haven't very much except the names of the various generals and admirals who were wounded.*[20]

And like Stauffenberg during the afternoon of 20th July 1944, Dulles still hopes that the rebellion against Hitler can gain more momentum. He cables another secret message in which he advocates the next steps the Allies should take to support the rebellion:

> 1. *Roosevelt should send a message to the German people in order to clear up any misunderstandings raised by the demand for unconditional surrender;*
> 2. *Berchtesgarden* [where Dulles mistakenly suspects Hitler to be] *should be massively bombarded in order to disrupt communications inside the Reich;*
> 3. *Any German cities that line up on the side of the opposition should be spared, while Nazi strongholds and Gestapo centres should be*

[20] C Mauch, *Shadow war against Hitler*, p. 118-119.

Other members of the Stauffenberg family were arrested including Berthold von Stauffenberg, the brother of Claus.

mercilessly bombarded;
4. Propaganda leaflets should be dropped over the entire territory of the Reich.[21]

But Dulles is clearly out of step with the general thinking in Washington and around the President. Roosevelt has no inclination to do any of the above. If there was indeed going to be a post-Hitler military junta governing Germany, they would probably demand a negotiated settlement. They would insist on certain members and institutions to stay in place. This in turn would frustrate FDR's stated aim to 'remake' post-war Germany from the ground up so that it could never threaten world peace again. This is not simply an official policy, this is a deeply held belief.

No other American President has had more early experience on German soil than FDR. His parents brought him eight times to Germany to take the cure at the famous health resort at Bad Nauheim. During these visits, young Franklin is enrolled into a local German school to improve his German. These first impressions form an opinion of Germany and the German people, which he holds true until the end of his life. For FDR, the German people are subjected to the rule of a military caste of Prussian

[21] C Mauch, op. cit., p. 119.

aristocrats who will forever harbour the desire for war. Already during the First World War FDR advocates unconditional surrender, in order for Germany's militarism to be cut down and purged. He tells the then President Wilson: The one lesson the German will learn is the lesson of defeat.[22]

When the news of the assassination attempt reaches America, reporters in San Diego badger the President's aides for the President's reaction to the news. FDR offers no comment on the 20th July, 1944. His secretary of State, Cordell Hull, is under strict instructions, the 'news about an attack on Hitler affords no particular basis for comment', is all the Press get. Only a week later, will Roosevelt make a first public statement about the assassination attempt and the army rebellion. Sitting with reporters on the emerald lawn of the Hawaiian governor's palace, he is excruciatingly careful, but he is clear that fighting will continue until Germany surrenders unconditionally:

> *I don't think I know any more about it than you do …. We can all have our own ideas about it. … Practically every German denies the fact they surrendered in the last war. But this time, they are going to know it!*[23]

At the Wolf's Lair, Adolf Hitler gets ready to broadcast to the nation. His secretary Christa Schroeder recalls the events:

> *During the evening a broadcasting van arrived from Königsberg and the broadcasting equipment was set up in the tea house. Shortly before midnight we walked with Hitler to the tea house. The officers injured in the attack were sitting there as well. Jodl had bandages around his head, Keitel's hands were in bandages. Shortly before midnight Hitler held his speech, it was a short speech to convince the German people that a great catastrophe had been avoided.*[24]

In a voice trembling with anger and emotion, Hitler records a fiery speech to the nation. The speech is broadcast ninety minutes later. Radios across the nation are switched on and in silence the nation hears Hitler's voice:

> *German men and women, …I address you today, so that you shall hear my voice and know that I am unhurt and alive, and so that you shall hear the details about a crime that has no equal in German history. An extremely small clique of ambitious, unscrupulous, foolish and criminally stupid officers hatched a plot to remove me. The bomb that was placed by Colonel von Stauffenberg exploded two metres away from me on my right side. It wounded very seriously many officers. I am entirely unhurt. …This I consider to be the confirmation of the task given to me by Providence, to*

[22] M Beschloss, op. cit., p. 9-12.
[23] M Beschloss, op. cit., p. 7.
[24] C Schroeder, *Er war mein Chef*, p. 149.

continue in pursuit of the aim of my life.[25]

Claus von Stauffenberg with three of his five children, and also a niece and nephew.

After the speech secretaries and leaders of the Reich congratulate Hitler once again for his miraculous survival. Assembled in the tea-house, Hitler and his entourage sit together until the early hours of the morning.[26]

Hitler's escape once more brings the entire German nation together. For weeks their fury against the plotters is said to be intense. It is reported that army officers in Berlin have to conceal their uniforms beneath raincoats to escape the people's indignation.[27]

Even Stauffenberg's eldest son, then eight years old and having been raised in Hitler Germany, can't believe that his hero father is behind the plot to kill Hitler:

> *I first realised that something was going on from reports on the wireless. My mother took us to our room to explain to us that it was our father who had placed the bomb to kill the Führer. My brother started crying violently and said how could he have done that? The Führer! But my mother said, that our father had thought that he must do this for Germany. We couldn't understand it. At school and in society we had grown up with Hitler he was almost godlike. How could our father have wanted to kill Hitler?*[28]

Treachery and treason become the only explanation for Hitler's military set-backs. The army's assassination attempt is a welcome

---

[25] M Domarus, *Hitler,* vol 2, p. 1219.

[26] T Junge, *Bis zur letzten Stunde,* p. 151.

[27] J Fest, op. cit., p. 281.

[28] Interview Count Berthold von Stauffenberg, Stauffenberg's eldest son, London, 13/03/2004.

Hitler broadcasting his speech to the German nation.

excuse to 'purge' the Wehrmacht. To restore the Führer's trust in the Wehrmacht, it is suggested during his lunchtime situation briefing on 22nd July, 1944, that the entire army will adopt the Hitler salute. The Führer signs the decree, but all the raised hands can not erase the cancer of suspicion and paranoia from Hitler's mind. After the 20th July, 1944, his security is heightened. Only 60 people now are allowed direct access to the Führer. All the others are being strip-searched. Attaché cases and luggage is no longer allowed into meetings with Hitler.[29]

It is around half an hour after midnight. The plot to kill Hitler is over. But the revenge has just begun.

By the night of 20th July, 1944, widespread manhunts are already under way. Besides those arrested in the Bendlerstrasse anyone who has had personal or professional contact with the known conspirators is rounded up. The Führer's rage is so immense that he decrees that the conspirators and their families should be eradicated:

> *My mother was taken away during the night. …I had heard whispers of concentration camps. …We never knew until after the war that all the grownups had gone to concentration camps.*[30]

Wives, brothers, sisters, aunts and uncles are taken away. Stauffenberg's wife Nina, heavily pregnant with the fifth child, is taken to Ravensbrück concentration camp. Her children – together with the children of the other conspirators – are taken away to an SS-run children's home. Forty-six children under sixteen years old, among them a ten week old baby, are told that

[29] I Kershaw, op. cit., p. 684. See also H Linge, *Bis zum Untergang*, p. 230-233.
[30] Interview Berthold von Stauffenberg, London 13/3/04.

The judge at the trial, Roland Freisler.

their parents are traitors and they will never see them again. They are forced to change their names. The aim is to re-educate them and place them with loyal, but childless SS families. Berthold von Stauffenberg and his siblings will only learn that their mother is alive after the liberation by the Allies in May 1945.[31]

More than 200 main conspirators are paraded in show trials in front of the People's Court. Hitler's special instructions for the judicial treatment of the accused are:

> *...the basest creatures that ever wore the soldier's tunic, this riff raff from a dead past. This time I'll fix them. There will be no honourable bullet for these criminals, they'll hang like common traitors! We'll have a court of honour dispel them from the armed services; then they can be tried by civilians ...the sentences will be carried out within two hours. They must hang at once, without any show of mercy![32]*

These trials begin on 7th August, 1944, in the great hall of the

[31] Ibid.
[32] J Fest, op. cit., p. 292.

Berlin People's Court. To humiliate the conspirators, they are forbidden to wear neckties, and Field Marshal von Witzleben is even forbidden to wear suspenders for his trousers. 'Judge' Roland Freisler opens the proceedings by heaping scorn on the accused, calling them rabble, criminals, traitors with the 'character of pigs'. Stauffenberg is called a 'criminal scoundrel'.[33]

On the afternoon of 8th August, 1944, immediately following their trials, the first group of condemned men is transported to the execution grounds in Ploetzensee Prison. Hitler has forbidden any spiritual consolation. SS men with floodlights storm into the cells and film the various prisoners. The resulting movie, an express wish of the Führer, is to show the entire process of the executions.[34]

The prisoners are allowed only enough time to change into prison garb. One by one they then cross the courtyard in wooden shoes, and enter the execution chamber. The executioners remove the prisoners' handcuffs, and place short, thin nooses around their necks and strip them to the waist. Hitler's wish is that they are strung up from piano wires. These executions are painfully long. Before the prisoner's death throes are over, the trousers are ripped off. Every detail is recorded on film, from the first wild struggle for breath to the final twitches. The film reels are sent to the Wolf's Lair where Hitler and some of his entourage watch them. Propaganda Minister Goebbels notes in his diary that he felt sick watching the film and had to leave the room.[35]

Hitler's revenge is excessive and barbarian – from the savage execution method to the broad sweep, even distant relatives of the mostly aristocratic conspirators fall victim to his lust for retribution.

Freisler reading the sentences on the plotters.

[33] J Fest, op. cit., p. 302.
[34] H Poelchau, *Die letzten Stunden*, p. 101.
[35] J Fest, op. cit., p. 303.

Almost 5000 men and women are tortured, arrested, put into concentration camps, killed, executed, or forced to commit suicide.

The 20th July, 1944, started with the prospect of killing Hitler and halting the war in Europe but ends in disaster for the German conspirators and the world at large. It is likely that Europe would have been spared a further ten months of slaughter, had Colonel Claus von Stauffenberg been successful.

But the tragedy of the failed generals is that by the summer of 1944 proving to the outside world, that there is indeed a better Germany, is almost more important than the success of their coup:

> *The assassination of Hitler must take place regardless. Even if it does not succeed, the coup d'état must be attempted. The point now is not the practical purpose, but to prove to the world and before history that the German resistance have staked their all and put their lives on the line. Besides that, nothing matters.*[36]

In fact the human cost of the failed assassination and ensuing army rebellion is enormous. More Germans will die between July 1944 and May 1945, than in the nearly five preceding war years.[37] Recent figures also suggest that the Nazi extermination machine in the concentration camps reaches fever-pitch only after August 1944 with a further two million men, women, and children perishing, probably because of the SS trying to kill off the evidence of their horrendous crimes in the concentration camps in view of the advancing Red Army.[38]

The 20th July, 1944, did change the course of the war – but not in the way Colonel Stauffenberg had hoped.

Having survived yet another attempt on his life, Hitler is now imbued with the conviction of his own religion. Until now he has listened very little to his military advisors, from now on he abandons all doubts in his own strategy and decides on more hopeless military campaigns. The German people will be submitted to an even more relentless propaganda campaign of 'total war'.

In the early hours of the 21st July, 1944 – in a final act of vengeance – the SS exhumes the body of Colonel von Stauffenberg. Stripped of his uniform and medals, his body is burnt. The ashes are dispersed on a field outside Berlin.

His own prediction has come tragically true:

> *If I succeed – they will call me a traitor to Germany.*
> *If I don't succeed – I will be a traitor to my own conscience.*

---

[36] H von Treschow in P Hoffmann, *Stauffenberg*, p. 248.
[37] 4.8 Million dead between July 1944 and May 1945, compared with 2.8 Million German soldiers and civilians dead between September 1939 and July 1944. J Fest, op. cit., p. 3
[38] I Kershaw, op. cit., p. 723.

APPENDIX

Making of Virtual History

By Jim Radford VFX The Moving Picture Company

O UR brief was to bring Churchill, Roosevelt and Hitler back to life, and re-create accurate archive footage from the 1940's.

This involved three main stages – recreate believable talking faces, integrate them into live action footage, and then to transform this into 'authentic' archive.

The following outlines the pipeline as applied to each of our characters.

Measurement

The 3D process started with the actor. Since we were creating only the face, as opposed to the whole head, the actor's head dimensions had to match those of the historical figures, in order to create a close fit between them.

Model

Once the actor was chosen, we took a plaster cast of his head. This was handed to a sculptor, who modelled the historical figure's face directly on the maquette. When this meticulous work was complete, the resultant plaster/clay model was laser-scanned, converting the physical model into computer data. This technique is very accurate, and ensures that the smallest physical detail is passed into the digital realm.

The face area was then extracted from this 3D model, and refined to create a workable mesh.

Texture

Next, using a wide range of detailed photographic reference, various layers or 'textures' were made, each representing a different aspect of the human face, these included colour, reaction to light (diffuse, specular and translucence), and skin detail (wrinkles, pores, distinguishing marks). These textures were mapped onto the 3D model, by degrees making the face more human. Lastly, the eyes, inside of the mouth, and facial hair were added, resulting in a static face that resembled our famous person.

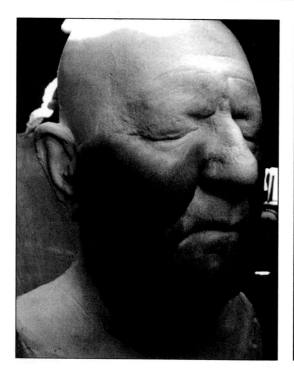 

Rig

The ensemble was made ready for animation. Our characters would not only have to display the full range of facial expression, but also deliver lines of dialogue. Whatever they were doing in the shots, they would have to remain believable.

(left) The plaster maquette with its initial modelling. (right) The clay model nearing completion.

Shoot

During the live action shoot, the actor wore a custom-made facial rig with markers attached, which allowed for the subsequent tracking of his head within the footage, and the replacement of his real face with the CG one. For each shot, the lighting setup and actor's backdrop were also recorded.

Mocap

After the live action, the actor was required to attend another shoot, this time concentrating on his facial movement. This Facial Motion Capture session involved the actor repeating his lines before camera, but this time with his skin painted with numerous dots. Every nuance of his facial movement was recorded. The human face can convey different emotions with the smallest of movements, and it was vital that we captured as much detail as possible.

Style and pace of delivery were also important here, as these had to conform to what was filmed on-set, so that the final shots remained coherent. The actor's performance was directed, and once on video the best takes were selected for processing.

Tracking & Lighting

Once the live action shots were digitised, the CG face was tracked onto the actor's head, and then lit to match the on-set lighting conditions. This involved reproducing the full lighting setup of the scene, including not only the main direct light sources, but also diffuse lighting effects, and any shadows cast by on-set objects.

Animation

Movement data from the Facial Motion Capture process was then applied, transforming the static face into a talking one, bringing the character alive.

One area of the face that required special attention was the character's eyes. When presented with a human face, be it in real life or photography, we 'zone-in' on the eyes, since it is this area that carries the most information – meaning, expression and emotion.

The actor, playing Churchill, wearing a custom-made facial rig with markers attached.

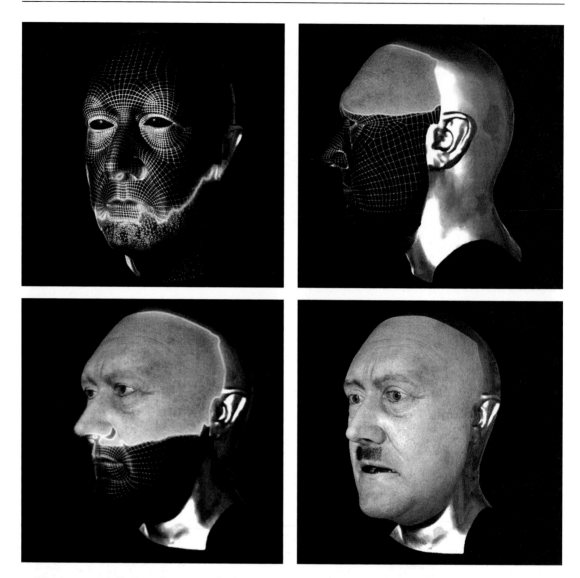

Having modelled and textured the eye area to a high degree, we animated eye direction, blinks and expressions. Different combinations of these resulted in radically different interpretations of the actor's performance.

Textures being mapped on to the 3D model.

Some of our best shots are, in my opinion, those where there is no dialogue, but where the actor's emotion is expressed solely through subtle eye movement and expression change.

Render

Once we were happy with the 3D look, we rendered the full-length shots. This involved calculating several different render 'layers', each representing a different aspect of the face – skin, eyes, mouth, hair etc.

The frames that make up the layers took anywhere from a couple of minutes to a couple of hours to compute, depending on the shot, generally, the bigger the face in frame, the longer the render time. Outputting these elements separately (as opposed to together in one image) facilitates the integration of the CG into the live action.

(above) The computer generated face intergrated with the actor's face using the grid 'markers' as the key. (below) The facial rig painted out.

Clean

For each shot, the practical facial rig worn by the actor was painted out, so as not to appear in the final sequence.

Integration

Starting with the live action background, the rendered layers were added, and their contribution to the image balanced, until the CG face blended seamlessly with the actor's head. It is only at this stage that shots visually come together, allowing the work to be evaluated, and if necessary, CG layers re-worked and re-integrated.

Archive

This stage was integral to the project. We needed to be able to play our shots alongside original archive footage and not be able to tell the difference.

We studied colour footage from the 1940's, and built up a 'life-story' for the exposed film through to the present day. From research into film stocks, development and printing techniques, and storage practices, we were able to isolate key visual clues, which we then applied to our contemporary footage, transforming it stage by stage into believable archive material.

Finally, film weave and jump cuts were added to complete the illusion.

Based on observation, and also to aid the viewer, we created a unique 'look' for each character. Our American, German and British looks displayed different colour slants and propensity to damage.

Conclusion

This project was a unique take on combining the old with the new. To use cutting-edge Visual Effects techniques to create imagery that supposedly originated decades before even the most basic CG was a fascinating premise.

Believable digital humans are arguably our industry's biggest challenge, and while there remains much work to do, we're very pleased with our results on this project.

Bibliography

All dates are for the editions used.

Alanbrooke, Field Marshal Lord, *War Diaries,* London 2003.
Alliluyeva, Svetlana, *Twenty Letters to a Friend,* London 1967.
Axell, Albert, *Stalin's War,* New York 1997.

Barnett, Correlli (Ed), *Hitler's Generals,* London 1990.
Below, Nicolaus von, *At Hitler's Side,* London 2001.
Beschloss, Michael, *The Conquerors,* New York 2002.
Bishop, Jim, *FDR's Last Year, April 1944-April 1945,* London 1975.
Black, Jeremy, *World War Two,* London 2003.
Bullock, Alan, *Hitler and Stalin,* London 1997.

Colville, John, *Downing Street Diaries 1939-1955,* London 1985.
Cooke, Neil, *interview 09/02/2004*

Dallek, Robert, *FDR and American Foreign Policy,* Oxford, 1979.
Delbars, Yves, *The Real Stalin,* London 1953.
Djilas, Milovan, *Conversations with Stalin,* New York 1962.
Domarus, Max, *Hitler. Reden und Proklamationen,* Wiesbaden 1973.
Dulles, Allen Welsh, *Germany's Underground,* London 2000.

Edmonds, Robin, *The Big Three,* London 1991.
Ellis, John, *One Day in a Very Long War,* London 1998.

FDR *Day By Day, The Pare Lorentz Chronology*
Ferrell, Robert H., *Choosing Truman,* Univ Missouri Press, 1994.
Ferrell, Robert H., *The Dying President,* London 1998.
Fest, Joachim, *Hitler. Eine Biographie,* Frankfurt 1979.
Fest, Joachim, *Plotting Hitler's Death,* London 1997.
Fest, Joachim, *interview 10/03/2004*

Gilbert, Martin, *Winston S Churchill, 8 vols,* London 1966-1988.
Gilbert, Martin, *Churchill a Life,* London 1991.
Goodwin, Doris Kearns, *No Ordinary Time,* New York 1994.

Hauner, Milan, *Hitler. A Chronology,* London 1983.
Hoffmann, Peter, *Hitler's Personal Security,* London 1979.
Hoffmann, Peter, *Stauffenberg A Family History,* London 2003.
Hyde, H Montgomery, *Stalin,* London 1971.

Irons, Roy, *Hitler's Terror Weapons,* London 2003.

Irving, David, *The Secret Diaries of Hitler's Doctor,* London 1990.

Junge, Traudl, *Bis zur letzten Stunde,* Munich 2002.

Keegan, John (Ed), *Churchill's Generals,* London 1991.
Keegan, John, *The Second World War,* London 1989.
Kershaw, Ian, *Hitler 1936-1945, Nemesis,* London 2000.
Kettenacker, Lothar, *The Other Germany in the Second World War,* Stuttgart 1977.
Kimball, Warren F., *Forged in War,* London 1997.
Kimball, Warren F., *The Juggler FDR as Wartime Statesman,* Princeton 1991
Kimball, Warren F., *interview 16/03/2004*
Krushchev, NS, *Krushchev Remembers,* London 1974.

Lamb, Richard, *Churchill,* London 1991.
Layton, Elizabeth (Nel), *Mr Churchill's Secretary,* London 1958.
Linge, Heinz, *Bis zum Untergang,* Munich 1980.

Mauch, Christof, *The Shadow War Against Hitler,* New York 2003.
Megargee, Geoffrey P., *Inside Hitler's High Command,* Univ of Kansas 2000.
Montefiore, Simon Sebag, *Stalin,* London 2004.

Neumaerker, Uwe; Conrad, Robert; Woywodt, Cord, *Wolfschanze,* Berlin 2000.

Puciato, Czeslaw, *Wolfsschanze,* London 1997.

Redlich, Fritz, *Hitler, Diagnosis of a destructive Prophet,* Oxford 1998.
Rigden, David, *Kill the Fuehrer,* London 1999.
Roberts, Andrew, *Hitler and Churchill,* London 2003.
Roosevelt, James, *My Parents. A differing view,* London 1977.

Schlabrendorf, Fabian von, *Offiziere gegen Hitler,* Berlin 1984.
Schmidt, Paul, *Statist auf diplomatischer Buehne,* Bonn 1953.
Schroeder, Christa, *Er war mein Chef,* Munich 1985.
Shtemenko, S M, *The Soviet general Staff at War 1941-1945,* Moscow 1981
Shukman, Harold (Ed), *Stalin's Generals,* London 1993.
Soames, Mary, *A Churchill Family Album,* London 1982.
Speer, Albert, *Inside the Third Reich,* London 1995.
Stalin's Appointments Book, Moscow, 1996.
Stauffenberg, Berthold Count von, *interview 10/03/2004*
Steinbach, Peter, *Lexikon des Widerstands,* Munich 1994.
Steinbach, Peter, *Widerstand in Deutschland,* Munich 1994.

Tagebuecher, *Die Tagebuecher von Joseph Goebbels 1941-1945, 15 vols,* Munich 1993-1998.
Tolland, John, *Adolf Hitler,* London 1977.

Ueberschaer, Gerd R. (Ed), *Der deutsche Widerstand gegen Hitler,* Stuttgart, 2001.

Volkogonov, Dmitri, *Stalin,* London 1991.

Ward, Geoffrey C., *A First Class Temperament,* New York 1989.
Warlimont, Walter, *Inside Hitler's Headquarters,* London 1964.

Zeller, Eberhard, *Oberst Claus Graf Stauffenberg,* Munich 1994.